*Integrating Individual
and Family Therapy*

BRUNNER/MAZEL INTEGRATIVE PSYCHOTHERAPY SERIES, NO. 4

# *Integrating Individual and Family Therapy*

## Larry B. Feldman, M.D.

BRUNNER/MAZEL *Publishers* · NEW YORK

*To my mother
Gertrude Feldman
and the memory of my father
Reuben Feldman*

Library of Congress Cataloging-in-Publication Data
Feldman, Larry B.
    Integrating individual and family therapy / by Larry B. Feldman.
        p.    cm. — (Brunner/Mazel integrative psychotherapy series; no. 4)
    Includes bibliographical references and index.
    ISBN 0-87630-623-7
    1. Psychotherapy patients—Family relationships. 2. Family
psychotherapy. 3. Psychotherapy.    I. Title. II. Series:
Brunner/Mazel integrative psychotherapy series : 4.
RC489.F33F45    1991
616.89′14—dc20                                                    91-25268
                                                                          CIP

*Published by*
BRUNNER/MAZEL, INC.
19 Union Square West
New York, New York 10003

MANUFACTURED IN THE UNITED STATES OF AMERICA

10  9  8  7  6  5  4  3  2  1

# *Contents*

*v*

# *Acknowledgments*

I would like to express my appreciation to those people who have helped me, directly and indirectly, during the process of writing this book:

My parents, Gertrude and Reuben Feldman, have provided loving support throughout my life.

My teacher, Chuck Kramer, introduced me to family therapy, encouraged my efforts to develop an integrative approach to working with couples and families, and provided a highly valued and respected role model.

My colleague and dear friend, Sandy Powell, read every word of every chapter, often more than once. Her highly insightful comments and consistent support have been of inestimable value.

John Norcross and Natalie Gilman have been extremely helpful editors. Their encouragement, patience, and specific suggestions are much appreciated.

My sons, Liam and Jonah, have been, and continue to be, sources of enormous pride and joy. They have been very supportive throughout the writing process.

Finally, I would like to express my appreciation to those

individuals and families with whom I have been privileged to work during the past 20 years, and to the many therapists whose work I have supervised during the past 15 years. The clinical examples in this book are all based on these experiences. Anonymity has been assured by means of widespread changes in regard to a great variety of descriptive characteristics. All of the names in all of the examples are fictitious.

# Introduction

Individual and family therapy have developed as separate, and often antagonistic, approaches to clinical work with children, adolescents, and adults. The rigid separation between these approaches has impaired therapists' ability to conduct comprehensive clinical assessments and to intervene in ways that promote both intrapsychic and interpersonal changes.

Integration of individual and family therapy concepts and techniques has the potential to markedly enhance clinical assessment and psychotherapeutic treatment of a wide range of emotional, behavioral, and family interactional problems (Feldman, 1976a, 1976b, 1976c, 1976d, 1979, 1982a, 1982b, 1985a, 1988, 1989; Feldman & Pinsof, 1982; Framo, 1981; Friedman, 1981; Gurman, 1981; Kramer, 1980; Lebow, 1984; Levant & Haffey, 1981; Malone, 1979; Moultrop, 1981; Nadelson, 1978; Pinsof, 1983; Sager, 1981; Sander, 1979; Segraves, 1982; Steinhauer, 1985; Sugarman, 1982; Wachtel & Wachtel, 1986; Walsh, 1983). In this book, a comprehensive model for integrating individual and family therapy will be described and application of the model will be extensively illustrated with clinical examples.

Initially, the focus will be on integrating individual and family systems conceptualizations of the etiology and maintenance of clinical problems. From an individually oriented perspective, clinical problems have been viewed as derivatives of intrapsychic processes (e.g., Carek, 1979; Luborsky, 1984; Meichenbaum, 1985). From a family-oriented perspective, primary emphasis has been placed on interpersonal processes (e.g., Aponte & VanDeusen, 1981; Barton & Alexander, 1981; Jacobson, 1981). There is considerable research evidence indicating that both intrapsychic and interpersonal processes are of major significance in the etiology and maintenance of a broad range of clinical problems experienced by (1) children and adolescents (Chamberlain & Steinhauer, 1983; Levine, Korenblum, & Golombek, 1983; McConville, 1983; Steinhauer & Berman, 1983); (2) adults (Babigian, 1985; Jaffe, 1985; Vaillant & Perry, 1985; Weissman & Boyd, 1985); (3) couples (Clifford & Kolodny, 1983; Rosenbaum & O'Leary, 1986); and (4) families (Kreindler & Armstrong, 1983; Robin & Foster, 1989). In light of this evidence, a comprehensive, multilevel model for integrating intrapsychic and interpersonal conceptualizations of clinical problems is clearly needed. Such a model is described in Chapter 1.

Based on an integrative, multilevel conceptualization of individual and family interactional problems, clinical assessment can be directed toward a clear delineation of the intrapsychic and interpersonal factors that are stimulating and maintaining those problems and of the intrapsychic and interpersonal strengths that are countering and limiting problem development. In making such an assessment, both conjoint and individual interviews are essential. Each type of interview has unique and complementary benefits and limitations. Conjoint interviews with couples, families, and family subgroups (e.g., parents) are uniquely valuable contexts for the direct observation of family interactional processes but are of limited value in regard to detailed exploration of individual family members' feelings and thoughts. Individual interviews, on the other hand, are ideal contexts for intrapsychic exploration but are quite limited in regard to identifying functional and dysfunctional family interactional patterns. Integration of conjoint and individual interviews enables the therapist to take advantage of the particular benefits of each format. In Chapter 2, a systematic method for integrating conjoint and individual assessment interviews is presented.

In addition to their complementary benefits and limitations in regard to clinical assessment, conjoint and individual interviews also have unique and complementary benefits and limitations in regard to therapeutic intervention. Conjoint interviews are particularly valuable contexts for the stimulation of interpersonal change processes because they allow the therapist to provide direct and immediate feedback to family members in response to functional and dysfunctional interactions and because they allow the family or family subgroup to practice new, more constructive ways of interacting in a safe and supervised arena. Individual interviews are particularly valuable contexts for the stimulation of intrapsychic change processes because they facilitate focused and in-depth exploration of conscious and unconscious emotional and cognitive processes and because they lower resistance to self-confrontation and self-modification. By combining conjoint and individual interviews, the therapist greatly enhances his or her ability to promote both interpersonal and intrapsychic changes. A method for systematically integrating these two types of treatment interviews is delineated in Chapter 3.

Therapeutic change has typically been conceptualized by individual psychotherapists in terms of processes for promoting intrapsychic changes (e.g., Carek, 1979; Luborsky, 1984; Meichenbaum, 1985) and by family therapists in terms of processes for promoting interpersonal changes (e.g., Aponte & VanDeusen, 1981; Gordon & Davidson, 1981; N. S. Jacobson, 1981). From an integrative, multilevel perspective, both intrapsychic and interpersonal change processes are highly significant. They are also complementary and synergistic. By developing an integrated approach, therapists can take advantage of the benefits of both types of change process, as well as the synergistic interactions between them. In Chapter 4, an integrative, multilevel model of therapeutic change is described.

In order to most effectively promote both intrapsychic and interpersonal changes, an integrated combination of individual and family therapy techniques is needed. Individually oriented techniques are the most effective means for promoting intrapsychic changes while family-oriented techniques are the most effective means for promoting interpersonal changes. Each type of technique enhances the effectiveness of the other. For instance, intrapsychically oriented work with a symptomatic individual often leads to the identification of areas of family dysfunction, which can then be explored in conjoint interviews utilizing family-oriented techniques. Conversely, efforts to promote changes in dysfunctional family interactions often lead to the identification of intrapsychic problems, which can then be explored in individual interviews by means of individually oriented techniques. Also, individual therapy techniques can be utilized in conjoint interviews to facilitate interpersonal change processes and family therapy techniques can be utilized in individual interviews to facilitate intrapsychic change processes. A systematic method for integrating individual and family therapy techniques is presented in Chapter 5.

In Chapter 6, potential problems that may be encountered during individual and family therapy integration are discussed, along with the most effective ways to avoid or overcome these problems. Here such issues as resistance to individual or conjoint interviews, complications in regard to confidentiality, lack of systematic treatment planning, loss of therapeutic balance, and failure to monitor the state of the therapeutic alliance with each family member are addressed.

Chapter 7 focuses on the phases of individual and family therapy integration. Each phase is described in terms of its goals, methods for achieving those goals, problems that may interfere with goal attainment, and methods for avoiding or overcoming such problems.

In Chapter 8, the concluding chapter, a review of the principles and methods of individual and family therapy integration is presented, along with a brief discussion of training in this approach.

Throughout the book, the importance of tailoring the structure and process of therapy to meet the particular needs of specific individuals and families is emphasized. Integration of individual and family therapy concepts, interview formats, and therapeutic techniques provides the therapist with a systematic and powerful method for accomplishing this objective.

# 1

## *Integrative Multilevel Conceptualization of Clinical Problems*

CLINICAL PROBLEMS have generally been conceptualized by individual psychotherapists in terms of intrapsychic processes (e.g., Beck, 1976; Berman, 1979; Kendall & Braswell, 1985; Luborsky, 1984) and by family therapists in terms of interpersonal processes (e.g., Aponte & Van-Deusen, 1981; Gordon & Davidson, 1981; Minuchin, 1974; Stanton, 1981). From an integrative, multilevel perspective, clinical problems are the result of both intrapsychic and interpersonal processes, along with the synergistic interactions between them. Ignoring or minimizing either level leads to an incomplete understanding of individual and family dysfunction.

The Integrative Multilevel Model (see Figure 1.1) combines and integrates the intrapsychic and interpersonal perspectives. The intrapsychic components of the model are derived from psychoanalytic and cognitive theory. The interpersonal components are derived from behavioral and family systems theory. In the following sections, the specific concepts from each of these theoretical frameworks will be

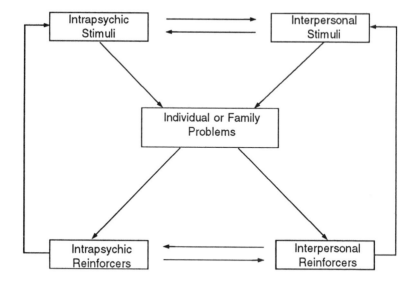

**Figure 1.1**
Integrative Multilevel Model

described. Subsequently, the integrative model will be presented and illustrated with clinical examples.

## THEORETICAL FRAMEWORKS

### Psychoanalytic Framework

From a psychoanalytic perspective, clinical problems are defensive reactions to unconscious anxiety (signal anxiety), defined as fear of unknown (i.e., unconscious) danger situations (S. Freud, 1926). In childhood, the major danger situations are interpersonal ones—disapproval, abandonment, or attack by significant others. Conscious and unconscious fantasies about these danger situations are present to some degree in all children, but they are especially strong when one or both parents have been unempathic, unavailable, neglectful, or abusive. Under these circumstances, a healthy sense of self-cohesion and self-esteem does not develop (Kohut, 1971, 1977). Instead, the self is experienced (consciously or unconsciously) as weak, helpless, worthless, or evil and thus vulnerable to rejection or attack by significant others.

As external relationships are internalized, anxiety is increasingly associated with internal representations of significant others and of the self in relation to these internalized others. Anxiety-generating fantasies are then projected into new relationships, such as those with teachers and peers. In adulthood, these fantasies are unconsciously transferred to current relationships, especially marital and family relationships.

In marital and family systems, anxiety generally takes one of two forms: fear of interpersonal closeness or fear of interpersonal distance. Fear of interpersonal closeness (intimacy anxiety) is manifested as a preconscious danger signal in response to actual or anticipated interpersonal closeness. In distressed families, this type of fear leads to dysfunctional distancing in marital and/or parent-child relationships. The nature and effects of intimacy anxiety are illustrated by the following examples.

*Clinical Illustrations*

(1) Each spouse in a conflictual marriage avoids initiating positive, intimacy-promoting interactions. This avoidance behavior is stimulated by each spouse's unconscious fear of interpersonal closeness. The husband fears that if he gets too close to his wife, he will be attacked by her. The wife fears that if she gets too close to her husband, she will be abandoned by him. Both spouses' fears are based, in part, on projection of unconscious introjects derived from experiences in their families of origin, where the husband was frequently denigrated by his mother and the wife was frequently ignored by her father.

(2) The father of a depressed boy spends little time with his son because he is unconsciously afraid that if he tries to have a close relationship with him, his wife will resent his "intrusion" into the extremely close relationship she has with the boy. This anxiety is derived, in part, from the father's experiences in his family of origin, where his mother was very possessive of him and often actively excluded his father from their relationship.

Fear of interpersonal distance (separation anxiety) is manifested as a preconscious danger signal in response to actual or anticipated interpersonal distance. In distressed families, this type of fear leads to inhibition of healthy autonomy in marital and/or parent-child relationships. The nature and effects of separation anxiety are illustrated by the following examples.

## Clinical Illustrations

(1) An agoraphobic woman is afraid to leave her house without being accompanied by her husband. Her fear is derived, in part, from experiences in her family of origin, where she was overprotected by her mother, who constantly warned her of the dangers of going out of the house alone and who reinforced her anxious, dependent behavior with excessive attention and concern.

(2) A school-phobic boy is afraid that if he goes to school something terrible might happen to his mother. This fear is based, in part, on projection of his unconscious hostility toward his mother, whom he experiences as withdrawn and unavailable. His symptom is a reaction to the anxiety generated by his unconscious hostility.

In order to prevent conscious experiencing of intense anxiety, defense mechanisms are created to block awareness of unconsciously perceived danger situations and of the thoughts and impulses (sexual, aggressive, or narcissistic) that are associated with these danger situations (A. Freud, 1933; S. Freud, 1926; Kohut, 1971). Defense mechanisms are thus a form of intrapsychic avoidance behavior.

By blocking conscious experiencing of anxiety, this avoidance behavior prevents emotional desensitization. It also prevents cognitive reappraisal of the unconsciously perceived danger situations that trigger the anxiety. As a result, there is a perpetuation of the anxiety, the defenses against the anxiety, and the unconscious perception of interpersonal danger (P. L. Wachtel, 1985). The following examples illustrate the role of defenses against anxiety in the generation of individual symptoms and dysfunctional family interactions.

## Clinical Illustrations

(1) A 15-year-old boy is in danger of being expelled from high school because he is failing most of his courses and he chronically disobeys the school rules. Clinical assessment reveals that his antisocial behavior is a defense against unconscious anxiety. Based on the difficulties he had with school work in elementary and junior high school, he is now afraid that he will be rejected by his high school peers because they will perceive him as stupid. In order to avoid this, he rejects school and seeks acceptance and admiration as an antisocial rebel. His anxiety is also derived from the frustration and rage that he feels about his inability to learn. His symptoms are, in part, a way of acting out these feelings and, in part, a plea for help in learning to control them.

(2) A conflictual couple are unable to sustain periods of positive relating. After one or two days of such relating, they begin arguing in increasingly destructive ways. Clinical assessment reveals that during the periods of positive relating, each spouse begins to unconsciously expect the other to say or do something hurtful. These unconscious expectations generate increasingly intense anxiety signals. To defend against this anxiety, both spouses become hypervigilant to anything in the other's behavior that could be construed as neglectful or critical. When one of them

perceives such behavior, he or she responds with verbal attacks on the other. These aggressive behaviors temporarily reduce their anxieties. At the same time, the other's aggressive behaviors are unconsciously interpreted as confirmatory evidence of each spouse's own initial negative expectations, thus reinforcing the vicious circle that repeatedly generates destructive arguing.

## Cognitive Framework

Cognitive theorists (e.g., Beck, 1976; Ellis, 1973; Meichenbaum, 1977) view clinical problems as primarily resulting from dysfunctional cognitions—that is, irrational or distorted perceptions, thoughts, expectations, and beliefs. Dysfunctional cognitions generally operate outside of conscious awareness but are capable of entering awareness with directed attention.

*Perceptual distortions* are inaccurate or incomplete perceptions of others, self, or the relationship between self and others. Such perceptions are partially accurate, but they are distorted by the mechanisms of magnification and minimization. Magnification is the process of perceiving the frequency, intensity, or importance of particular behaviors, thoughts, or feelings as greater than it actually is. Minimization is the opposite of magnification—that is, the frequency, intensity, or importance of particular behaviors, thoughts, or feelings is perceived as less than it actually is. Usually these two forms of perceptual distortion operate together.

*Clinical Illustrations*

(1) The mother of a school-phobic girl magnifies her daughter's expressed anxiety and minimizes her coping capacities. As a result, she perceives her as terrified, helpless, and fragile when, in reality, she is frightened but capable of effective coping.

(2) The husband and wife in a conflictual marriage each perceive him- or herself as the "innocent victim" of an inconsiderate, selfish spouse. While these perceptions are not totally false, they are distorted by magnification of the other's negative behavior and of each one's own positive behavior and by minimization of the other's positive behavior and of each one's own negative behavior.

*Dysfunctional thoughts* ("automatic thoughts"; "dysfunctional self-statements") are thoughts about self or others that distort reality by means of overgeneralization (drawing a generalized conclusion from a specific, limited experience), arbitrary inference (inferring a specific conclusion on the basis of minimal evidence), or catastrophic projection (assuming that noncatastrophic events will have catastrophic consequences). Examples of dysfunctional automatic thoughts are (1) A depressed adolescent boy responds to any setback or failure with the automatic thought, "I'm never successful at anything"; (2) An agoraphobic woman begins to feel anxious and thinks, "I'm going to die"; (3) The husband of an agoraphobic woman reacts to any sign of anxiety in his wife with the thought, "She needs my help"; and (4) The wife in a distressed marriage reacts to any form of inconsiderate behavior by her husband with the thought, "This is absolutely intolerable."

Perceptual distortions and dysfunctional self-statements are derived, in part, from *unrealistic expectations*. These are rigid, arbitrary, or irrational expectations of self, others, or relationships. Examples of unrealistic expectations are "I should always get perfect grades in school"; "My wife should know what my feelings are without my having to tell her"; "Our family should never have any disagreements."

Unrealistic expectations are based on *irrational beliefs* —that is, implicit assumptions about self, others, or relationships that are derived from irrational premises. Examples of such beliefs are "If I am not perfect, I am worthless"; "If you really love someone, you can tell what he or she is feeling just by looking at him or her"; "A happy family doesn't have disagreements."

### Behavioral Framework

From a behavioral perspective, individual and family interactional problems are primarily the result of interpersonal problem stimulation and problem reinforcement processes (Goldfried & Davison, 1976; Gordon & Davidson, 1981; N. S. Jacobson, 1981). Interpersonal problem stimuli are behaviors by one or more individuals that lead to the arousal of dysfunctional cognitions, emotions, and behaviors in one or more other individuals. Interpersonal problem reinforcers are behavioral reactions by one or more individuals to dysfunctional behavior by one or more other individuals that have the effect of increasing the probability of recurrence of the dysfunctional behavior.

*Interpersonal problem stimulation* is often derived from a low level of positive responsiveness by one or more individuals to constructive behavior by one or more other individuals. The lack of positive responsiveness is frustrating and, over time, demoralizing. These emotional reactions then lead to dysfunctional behavior.

## Clinical Illustrations

(1) The parents of an underachieving boy do not praise him for his positive accomplishments because they want him to "work to his potential." The lack of reinforcement discourages him from trying to improve his performance.

(2) Each spouse in a conflictual marriage ignores the positive, intimacy-promoting behaviors of the other because each one is "sure it won't last." As a result, the frequency of positive behavior diminishes and the frequency of negative, hostile behavior increases.

Interpersonal problem stimulation also occurs when individuals are not clear, congruent, or consistent in their communications with each other.

## Clinical Illustrations

(1) The parents of a 9-year-old boy with behavior control problems are inconsistent in their communication of expectations. One day they tell him that he is not allowed to

watch television for more than an hour; the next day they allow him to watch television for three hours. The lack of consistency in the parents' expectations contributes to the lack of consistency in their son's behavior.

(2) The spouses in a conflictual marriage do not discuss their expectations of each other because each one believes that the other should "know" what he or she wants without having to spell it out. As a result, each spouse frequently behaves in ways that the other experiences as thoughtless and hurtful.

A third major source of interpersonal problem stimulation is aversive behavior by one or more individuals toward one or more other individuals. The most extreme form of aversive stimulation is physical or sexual abuse. In recent years, it has become clear that these forms of trauma occur much more often than was formerly believed and are associated with a wide variety of individual and interactional problems (Finkelhor, 1984; Kempe & Kempe, 1978). In addition to physical or sexual abuse, verbal abuse is a common interpersonal problem stimulus. Verbal abuse may take the form of yelling, sarcasm, generalized criticisms, put-downs, or name-calling. These behaviors stimulate feelings of hurt and anger and lead to escalating spirals of dysfunctional interaction.

More subtle, but equally significant, forms of aversive stimulation are overintrusiveness and overprotectiveness. These behaviors inhibit the development of autonomy and self-esteem and stimulate excessive dependency and separation anxiety (Williams, Berman, & Rose, 1987).

Aversive stimulation may result from direct interaction between two or more individuals or it may be the result of one individual observing aversive interactions between two or more other individuals. For example, children in dysfunctional families are indirectly affected by observing the dysfunctional interactions of their parents.

*Interpersonal problem reinforcement* occurs when one or more individuals react to dysfunctional behavior by one or more other individuals in such a way that the probability of the dysfunctional behavior recurring is increased. Interpersonal reinforcement may be either positive (provision of a reward) or negative (removal of an aversive stimulus). Both types of reinforcement are illustrated in the following example.

## Clinical Illustration

A mother and her 5-year-old son are shopping at the grocery store. The boy grabs a candy bar, asking his mother if he can have it. She says no and he begins yelling at her and kicking the grocery cart. She says, "O.K., you can have the candy bar." He immediately stops his tantrum, gives her a big hug, and says, "Thank you, mommy." In this example, the boy's tantrum behavior is being positively reinforced by his mother's acquiescent response. The mother's acquiescent response is being negatively reinforced by the cessation of her son's tantrum behavior and positively reinforced by his hug and expression of thanks.

*Punishing* consequences are behavioral reactions by one or more people to the behavior of one or more other people that have the effect of decreasing the probability that the punished behavior will recur. Effective use of appropriate punishment in response to dysfunctional behavior reduces the likelihood of recurring behavior. For instance, if the mother in the grocery store example had responded to her son's tantrum behavior with a clear, firm communication that he must stop yelling and kicking and that there will be no treats of any kind until he does, the likelihood of the tantrum behavior continuing would have diminished. Her failure to implement such consequences contributed to the continuation of the problem and increased the probability that the same problem will recur in the future.

The reinforcing or punishing quality of a reaction to dysfunctional behavior is not always apparent from the appearance of the reaction. For example, under certain conditions an ostensibly punishing reaction—yelling, for instance—may function as a behavioral reinforcer because the attention that accompanies the reaction is sufficiently rewarding to offset its aversive qualities. Behavioral consequences are operationally defined as reinforcing or punishing by the effects they have on the recipient of the consequence, not by the desired intentions of the provider.

## Family Systems Framework

Family systems theory views clinical problems primarily in terms of dysfunctional patterns of family interaction. The major conceptual categories used to analyze the nature of these dysfunctional interactional patterns are family rules, family homeostasis, and family structure (Feldman, 1976a; Feldman & Pinsof, 1982).

*Family rules* are conscious or unconscious agreements that prescribe and limit family members' behavior (Jackson, 1965). These rules define a range of acceptable behavior for individual family members and for the family as a whole. When one or more family members deviate from the rule-defined limits, homeostatic negative feedback mechanisms are activated. These are behaviors by one or more family members that have the effect of bringing the family system back within its rule-defined permissible deviation limits.

In dysfunctional family systems, clinical problems often function as negative feedback mechanisms. For example: (1) A child's symptomatic behavior increases when the conflict level between the parents starts to escalate; (2) Whenever the level of intimacy becomes too great in a conflictual marriage, a dysfunctional conflict is triggered; (3) A wife becomes depressed when the level of tension in her marriage becomes too great.

In contrast to negative feedback, which is deviation-counteracting, positive feedback is deviation-amplifying (Maruyama, 1968). When the amplified deviations are constructive ones, positive feedback brings about growth and adaptive change. When the deviations are destructive, positive feedback leads to problem escalation.

Families who seek therapy are generally stuck in a maladaptive pattern of negative-feedback-regulated homeostasis. These families are fearful (consciously or unconsciously) of the possibility of destructive problem escalation. The decision to seek therapy is often precipitated by a sudden or gradual increase in the frequency and/or intensity of clinical problems, which triggers fears of an uncontrollable process of problem escalation.

*Family structure*, defined as the manner in which the relationships among family members are organized (Aponte & VanDeusen, 1981; Minuchin, 1974), provides another useful way of viewing family interactional patterns. Family structure has been conceptualized primarily in terms of family boundaries and family roles.

*Family boundaries* are the functional characteristics that distinguish the family from its social environment and that distinguish family subgroups and individual family members from each other. In dysfunctional families, such boundaries are often either overly rigid or overly diffuse. Families with overly rigid boundaries ("disengaged families") are characterized by a lack of interrelatedness and interdependency among family members and family subsystems. In these families, individuals function autonomously without a sense of family cohesion or family support. Families with overly diffuse boundaries ("enmeshed families") are characterized by a lack of separation and individuation among family members and family subsystems. In these families, there is a high degree of togetherness along with a low degree of differentiation (Bowen, 1978).

In many families, the structure is a combination of disengagement and enmeshment. For instance, a mother and father may be disengaged while mother and daughter are enmeshed. Similarly, a couple may be disengaged from each other but enmeshed with their families of origin.

In families with symptomatic children or adolescents, the symptoms are often related to family structural problems. For example, a child whose parents are disengaged may become symptomatic in response to a conscious or unconscious desire to bring them together. On the other hand, in a family where the child is enmeshed with one or both parents, the symptoms may function as a means for achieving some degree of separation and individuation.

Symptomatic spouses are also often responding to structural stresses in their relationship. For example: (1) Depressed individuals frequently have marriages characterized by a high degree of hostile disengagement (Canetto, Feldman & Lupei, 1989; Weissman & Paykel, 1974); (2) Agoraphobic individuals often have enmeshed marriages in which their autonomous functioning is inhibited (Hafner, 1986); and (3) Many conflictual couples become disengaged in response to conscious or unconscious fear of becoming enmeshed (Feldman, 1979).

*Family roles* are recurrent patterns of family interaction that reflect conscious and unconscious expectations of how particular family members should and should not behave. There are two major types of family role expectations—positional and individual. Positional expectations define appropriate and inappropriate behavior for particular family positions—husband, wife, father, mother, son, daughter. These expectations are derived from two major sources: (1) modeling and conditioning within the family of origin; and (2) modeling and conditioning outside of the family, such as by television, movies, advertisements, and so forth. Gender role conditioning, inside and outside of the family, is a major source of positional family role expectations (Feldman, 1982b).

Individual role expectations define appropriate and inappropriate behavior for particular family members rather than particular family positions. For example, in families in which one parent is an alcoholic, the other parent is often in a codependent role, with one or more of the children often in the role of parental child (Wegscheider, 1981).

Positional and individual role expectations contribute to the development of clinical problems when they are overly rigid or overly diffuse. Overly rigid role expectations inhibit individual development and block flexible family functioning. Overly diffuse role expectations blur the distinctions between different family positions (e.g., parent and child) or different family members (e.g., older child and younger child) and thereby lead to role or identity diffusion (Erikson, 1963; Haley, 1976).

## INTEGRATION

The Integrative Multilevel Model, graphically represented in Figure 1.1 (see p. 4), combines and integrates the psychodynamic, cognitive, behavioral, and family systems perspectives. In the following sections, the nature of this integration will be described and illustrated with clinical examples.

### Intrapsychic and Interpersonal Problem Stimulation

Dysfunctional behaviors are stimulated intrapsychically by conscious and preconscious dysphoric emotions (fear, sadness, guilt, shame, rage, etc.). These emotions are aroused by preconscious perceptual and cognitive distortions. The latter processes are stimulated by unconscious (signal) anxiety. Signal anxiety is derived from unconscious conflicts and irrational beliefs. Thus, unconscious, preconscious, and conscious cognitions and emotions interact in a mutually causal spiral, eventuating in dysfunctional behavior.

At the interpersonal level, emotional and behavioral problems are stimulated, directly or indirectly, by the behaviors of other family members. These behaviors may take the form of excessively rigid or excessively permeable boundaries or roles; insufficient reinforcement of constructive behavior; unclear or inconsistent communication; overprotective or overintrusive behavior; or verbal, physical, and/or sexual abuse.

Intrapsychic and interpersonal problem stimulation processes interact in a reciprocal, circular pattern. Family members' dysfunctional behaviors are most directly stimulated by their conscious, preconscious, and unconscious cognitions and emotions. These intrapsychic stimuli are themselves stimulated, in part, by the interpersonal behaviors of other family members. The behaviors of these other family members are responses to their conscious, preconscious, and unconscious cognitions and emotions which are, in part, stimulated by the interpersonal behaviors of the originally described family member or members. This pattern is illustrated by the following clinical examples.

## Clinical Illustrations

(1) A 10-year-old girl, Alice, and her parents came for an evaluation because of the parents' concern about Alice's intense fear of being separated from them. Whenever the

parents tried to leave her with someone else at night, she became extremely distraught. She was also afraid to sleep over at any of her friends' houses, consistently refusing their invitations to do so. As a result, she was starting to lose her friends.

Clinical assessment revealed that Alice's symptomatic behaviors were being stimulated by her conscious fear that something terrible might happen to her if she were separated from her parents. Underlying this conscious fear was the preconscious belief that if she were separated from her mother, she or her mother might die. This belief had been aroused, in part, by her mother's depression and emotional withdrawal following the death of her own mother six months prior to the emergence of Alice's symptoms. Currently it was being stimulated by her mother's overly protective behavior. For instance, she frequently reminded Alice to be careful, asked her repeatedly if she felt afraid, and organized her time so that Alice was seldom left alone. This problem-stimulating behavior by Alice's mother was a response to her own (the mother's) conscious and unconscious anxiety. The major stimuli for this anxiety were her unconscious conflicts (particularly those connected with her own mother) and Alice's symptomatic behavior.

The father's symptom-stimulating behavior took the form of frequent outbursts of verbally expressed anger toward both Alice and her mother. These outbursts contributed to Alice's fear that if her parents left her alone, she or her mother might die.

(2) Barbara and Bill came for marital therapy because of increasingly frequent destructive arguments, characterized by mutual blaming, name-calling, and threats of divorce.

These arguments usually began when Barbara became angry with Bill in response to certain behavior that she experienced as inconsiderate and hurtful (e.g., coming home late and not calling). She responded with verbal hostility, such as, "You are a self-centered, inconsiderate bastard." He felt hurt by this and withdrew into a cold, distant silence. Barbara reacted to this behavior with even more anger and more verbal hostility. At that point, Bill would respond with hostile and demeaning comments about Barbara. From there on, the argument became increasingly more dysfunctional. Eventually, they withdrew from each other and maintained a "cold war" atmosphere for hours to days. After a time, one of them made an initiative designed to stimulate a reconciliation. Sometimes, this initiative was rejected, leading to another round of arguing. More often, the other responded positively and they entered a short-lived period of nonhostile relating.

Clinical assessment revealed that Barbara and Bill's dysfunctional conflicts were stimulated at the interpersonal level by Bill's passive-aggressive behavior and by Barbara's verbally aggressive behavior. Once the conflicts began to escalate, each person's hostile and demeaning behavior elicited similar behavior by the other. Intrapsychically, their conflicts were stimulated by both spouses' unrealistic expectations and feelings of narcissistic vulnerability. Each of them unconsciously expected the other to be immediately and totally responsive to his or her wishes and felt needs. Barbara expected Bill to be thoughtful and considerate at all times and was highly threatened when he wasn't. Bill expected Barbara to be admiring and affirming at all times and was highly threatened when she wasn't. When expectations were frustrated, each one felt enormously hurt and vulnerable. Barbara defended against her feelings of vulnerability by verbally attacking Bill. He initially defended himself by withdrawing into a cold, hostile shell; but when he was sufficiently aroused, he also became verbally aggressive.

Each spouse's behavior triggered the other's most painful anxieties. Barbara felt most afraid of being abandoned. Bill's passive-aggressive behavior was a potent stimulus of this anxiety. Bill's most central fear was that he would be attacked. Barbara's criticisms were powerful elicitors of this anxiety. Each spouse's defenses against his or her own anxiety further aroused the anxiety of the other. Barbara defended against her fear of abandonment by criticizing Bill. This behavior aroused Bill's fear of attack, leading him to withdraw from Barbara. His withdrawal further aroused her fear of abandonment, triggering more criticism from her and more withdrawal from Bill. Eventually, they both became verbally abusive, leading to an escalating spiral of dysfunctional conflict (Feldman, 1982a).

### Intrapsychic and Interpersonal Problem Reinforcement

Clinical problems are reinforced intrapsychically by the temporary anxiety reduction and impulse gratification that they produce. The anxiety reduction is negatively reinforcing (removal of an aversive stimulus) while the impulse gratification is positively reinforcing (provision of a reward). These intrapsychic reinforcing consequences contribute to the continuation of dysfunctional behavior by increasing the likelihood that such behavior will recur under similar stimulus conditions in the future. They also contribute to the persistence of the underlying conflicts, anxieties, and cognitive distortions that stimulate such behavior because they decrease the likelihood that these processes will enter conscious awareness, where they could be reduced via emotional desensitization and cognitive reappraisal.

At the interpersonal level, clinical problems are reinforced by the interactional consequences that they produce. These consequences may take the form of a positive reward (attention, praise, nurturance, etc.) or they may consist of the removal of a negative aversive stimulus (crying, yelling, hitting, etc.). Both types of reinforcement increase the likelihood that the problem behaviors will recur under similar stimulus conditions in the future.

Intrapsychic and interpersonal problem reinforcers interact in an additive way. The most immediate reinforcement occurs at the intrapsychic level, often outside of conscious awareness. This is soon followed by interpersonal reinforcement, as family members respond to the problem behavior. These responses are reinforcing by virtue of their intrapsychic effects; that is, they lead to temporary anxiety reduction and/or impulse gratification. Thus, there is an additive interaction between the direct effects of intrapsychic reinforcement and the indirect effects of interpersonal reinforcement. This interaction is illustrated by the following continuations of the previous clinical examples.

## Clinical Illustrations

(1) At the intrapsychic level, Alice's symptoms produced a temporary decrease in her conscious anxiety. They also produced some degree of unconscious gratification of her dependent wishes. These effects were directly reinforcing.

Alice's symptoms were reinforced at the interpersonal level by her parents' reactions to her symptomatic behavior. Alice's parents attempted to cope with her separation anxiety by delaying or canceling their plans so that they could comfort her. If they did go out, they called in at frequent intervals to make sure that she was alright. When they called, she would cry hysterically, begging them to come home. Usually, they complied with her request. These behaviors reinforced Alice's symptoms because they led to a temporary decrease in her level of conscious anxiety and because they provided a good deal of attention and nurturant gratification. At the same time, they promoted the continuation of her unconscious anxiety by preventing her from learning that her fantasies about the disastrous consequences of separation were unrealistic.

(2) The dysfunctional conflicts between Bill and Barbara were reinforced at the intrapsychic level by a temporary reduction in each person's feelings of narcissistic vulnerability and by gratification of their aggressive impulses. Interpersonally, their conflict behaviors were reinforced by the attention that each one elicited from the other and by the coercion-induced compliance (giving in for the purpose of ending the argument) that sometimes occurred. These interpersonal reactions led to short-term benefits—tem-

porary cessation of conflict—but at the same time, they contributed to each spouse's avoidance of conscious confrontation with the underlying feelings of vulnerability that repeatedly triggered new episodes of conflict.

## Implications for Clinical Assessment

The Integrative Multilevel Model highlights the importance of both intrapsychic and interpersonal factors in the stimulation and reinforcement of clinical problems. Based on this model, comprehensive clinical assessment is directed toward identification of both intrapsychic and interpersonal problem stimulation and problem reinforcement processes, along with the interactions between them. In the following chapter, a method for conducting such an integrative assessment will be described.

# 2

*Integrating Individual
and Family Assessment*

INTEGRATIVE MULTILEVEL assessment is directed toward the development of a comprehensive understanding of individual and family interactional problems and strengths and toward the establishment of positive working alliances with individual family members, family subgroups, and the family as a whole. In conducting such an assessment, both conjoint and individual interviews are essential. Each of these formats has specific benefits and limitations. By utilizing an integrated combination of both types of interviews, their particular benefits can be combined to produce a more accurate and comprehensive assessment than would be possible with either format alone. In the following sections, the benefits and limitations of conjoint and individual interviews will be delineated and a method for integrating these formats will be described.

## CONJOINT INTERVIEWS

### Benefits

Conjoint interviews with couples, families, and family subgroups (e.g., parents, siblings) are uniquely valuable contexts for the assessment of interpersonal problems and strengths and interpersonal problem stimulation and problem reinforcement processes. They are also uniquely valuable contexts for the establishment of positive working alliances between the therapist and the family group and between the therapist and relevant family subgroups. By meeting with family members together, the therapist is able to join with them in a collaborative effort to understand and change their dysfunctional behaviors and interactional patterns.

In a conjoint interview, the therapist is able to observe how family members organize themselves (who sits next to whom, who speaks to whom, etc.); their postures, gestures, and facial expressions; and the quality, pitch, and loudness of their voices. Sequences of nonverbal and verbal behavior are valuable sources of insight into the ways in which family members consciously and unconsciously stimulate and reinforce each other (e.g., husband moves back in his chair when his wife begins to talk about their sexual problems; son interrupts when mother and father begin to argue; father answers a question addressed to daughter; etc.). Equally valuable are the therapist's observations of the similarities and differences among each family member's perceptions of the problems and strengths in the family and of the constructive and destructive ways that family members discuss the problems that they have identified.

Another major benefit of conjoint interviews is that they provide an opportunity for consensual clarification of self-reported behaviors and behavior sequences. Often, family members remember the same events in quite different ways. For example, a husband may report that he drinks once or twice a week, while his wife states that he drinks every day. Similarly, a teenage boy may indicate that his behavior in school is "great," but his mother reports that she is receiving frequent complaints from his teacher about his behavior. Clarification of these differences is essential for the development of an accurate assessment.

In addition to their value as contexts for assessing interpersonal problems and strengths, conjoint interviews are also valuable sources of information about individual problems and strengths and intrapsychic problem stimulation and reinforcement processes. Observing individuals in the context of their family provides a unique perspective from which to formulate hypotheses about intrapsychic dynamics. These hypotheses can then be investigated more thoroughly in the context of individual interviews.

## Limitations

One of the limitations of conjoint assessment interviews is that family members are often unwilling to raise or discuss important issues concerning themselves, other family members, or interactions among family members. Examples of such issues are suicidal ideation, feelings of worthlessness or hopelessness, thoughts about divorce, homosexual impulses or behavior, alcohol or drug abuse, marital violence, extramarital affairs, and physical or sexual child abuse. When the therapist's assessment does not include a detailed understanding of such feelings, thoughts, and behaviors, that assessment will be incomplete in important areas. In some instances, for example, when a family member is suicidal or when a child is being physically or sexually abused, it may be dangerously incomplete.

A second limitation of conjoint assessment interviews is that the therapist is not able to observe and interact with individual family members outside of the context of their family. Often, the behavior and demeanor of spouses, children, and parents are strikingly different in an individual interview from that seen in a conjoint interview. For example, a person who looks and acts anxious or depressed in the context of his or her family may be much calmer or brighter in an individual interview. Conversely, someone who looks relatively healthy in a conjoint interview may manifest a great deal of anxiety or depression in an individual interview. If the therapist only observes family members in the context of conjoint family interviews, his or her assessment will be markedly incomplete.

## INDIVIDUAL INTERVIEWS

### Benefits

Individual interviews with children, adolescents, and adults are uniquely valuable contexts for the assessment of intrapsychic problems and strengths and intrapsychic problem stimulation and reinforcement processes. They are also uniquely valuable contexts for the establishment of positive working alliances between the therapist and individual family members. These interviews allow the therapist to observe and interact with individuals separate from their family system, providing an opportunity for detailed exploration of feelings, thoughts, and behaviors, including those that individual family members would not be willing to discuss in a conjoint family interview.

In an individual interview, the therapist is able to focus intensively and extensively on individual family members' feelings and thoughts about the presenting problems, their marital or family relationships, and themselves. The privacy of the individual setting reduces defensiveness and facilitates disclosure of information about self or others that family members may be too fearful, guilty, or ashamed to bring up in a conjoint family interview. Discussion of such issues in individual interviews is essential for the development of a comprehensive assessment.

In addition to their value as contexts for the assessment of intrapsychic problems and strengths, individual interviews are also valuable sources of hypotheses about interpersonal problems and strengths and interpersonal problem stimulation and reinforcement processes. Once formulated, these hypotheses can then be explored in subsequent conjoint interviews.

## Limitations

The major limitations of individual interviews are that they do not provide direct access to family interactions, they do not provide an opportunity for consensual validation, and they do not allow the therapist to observe individuals in the context of their family. As noted earlier, the differences between how an individual behaves when seen alone and how he or she behaves while interacting with his or her family can be dramatic. When the therapist's observations are limited to individual interviews, a great deal of important information will be missing.

Another potential limitation of individual interviews is that people may reveal information about self or others that is not known to other family members or that one or more family members do not want revealed to anyone outside of the family. If the therapist has not clearly communicated his or her position in regard to confidentiality, this situation can become problematic. Therefore, it is essential that the therapist discuss confidentiality at the beginning of all initial individual and family subgroup interviews.

## CONFIDENTIALITY

Confidentiality can be dealt with in a number of different ways. Each approach has specific advantages and disadvantages. Therapists need to decide which approach they are most comfortable with, communicate this approach at the outset, and then apply the approach consistently throughout the assessment and subsequent therapy.

## The Therapist's Confidentiality

The first issue that the therapist needs to discuss is whether or not he or she will maintain confidentiality. One approach is for the therapist to take the position that confidentiality cannot be maintained because the assessment includes both individual and conjoint interviews. The therapist states that in order to be helpful, he or she must be free to share with the other members of the family any information that is revealed in an individual interview. This position avoids the possibility of learning about "secrets" that cannot be shared and therefore may be disruptive of the therapy. However, it places serious limits on the willingness of many individuals to discuss important issues.

A second approach is to take the position that confidentiality will be maintained as long as doing so would not endanger anyone's safety. This position maximizes the likelihood that individuals will share important information. It also leaves the door open to learning about "secrets" that cannot be brought up with other family members. The two most effective ways of dealing with this potential problem are (1) to state that while confidentiality will be maintained, the therapist may at times encourage individuals themselves to share particular information with other family members; and (2) to indicate that from time to time the therapist may ask permission to share with one or more other family members information revealed in an individual interview.

A good rule of thumb is that disclosure is necessary when the therapist believes that effective therapy will be impossible unless he or she is able to discuss the information that has been revealed with the other family members. When disclosure is recommended, it is essential that the therapist thoroughly explore the individual's feelings about disclosure by self or by therapist to other family members. The following examples illustrate instances when the therapist decided that disclosure was necessary.

## Clinical Illustrations

(1) A wife revealed in an individual interview that her husband had been physically abusive to her in the past. Because it was essential for the therapist to discuss this with the husband, the husband needed to be told that she had revealed this information. The wife was asked if she felt that such a disclosure might be dangerous for her (she did not) and whether she would rather share the information herself or have the therapist do so (she preferred to share the information herself). The husband was embarrassed about his wife's disclosure but was willing to discuss his feelings and thoughts about his previous violent behavior and to make a commitment to resolve all future disputes in nonviolent ways.

(2) A husband revealed that his business was deeply in debt and that he was embarrassed to tell his wife about it. He was urged to reveal this information to his wife so that

the two of them could discuss the implications for them and their children. He was initially resistant to this suggestion, but after some discussion he did agree to tell his wife. When he did so, she reacted with anger. Soon, however, she was able to engage with him in a constructive dialogue about strategies for dealing with their financial problem.

(3) A 13-year-old boy revealed in an individual interview that he and some friends had been playing with firecrackers in potentially dangerous ways. He was told that either he or the therapist had to tell his parents about this behavior. On hearing this, he became quite angry but seemed relieved when the information was revealed in the next conjoint interview.

(4) A 17-year-old girl revealed that she was bulimic. She had not told her parents about her bulimia because she didn't want to worry them. She was told that telling her parents would be helpful to her and to them because they would be less worried about a known problem than they already were about an unknown one. She chose to reveal the information herself. The disclosure did, in fact, worry the parents initially and they asked a great many questions about their daughter's illness. Once they had the information, however, their anxiety was reduced and they were able to support her efforts to control her binging and purging.

In many instances, disclosure to other family members is *not* necessary. Effective therapy does not require that every family member be aware of everything that the therapist hears from every other family member. Even when the therapist learns something that other family members are not aware of, disclosure still may not be necessary. The deciding criterion is whether or not the lack of disclosure would disrupt the therapeutic process or would be unethical. Often, neither is the case. The following examples illustrate instances when the therapist decided that disclosure was not necessary.

### Clinical Illustrations

(1) A wife revealed that she had had a series of extramarital affairs during the course of her marriage. She had not disclosed any of these affairs to her husband and did not want to disclose them. She currently was committed to working on her marriage and to maintaining a monogamous relationship with her husband during this process. The therapist decided that disclosure was not necessary in order for him to work with this couple. The question of whether or not to disclose the affairs at some future time was left for the wife to decide.

(2) A husband revealed that without telling his wife, he had sent money to his son from a former marriage. Previously, his current wife had expressed strong opposition to such action. The husband said that he did not plan to send any more money and that he didn't want his wife to know about the money he had sent. The amount of money was not large and presented no threat to the family's finances. The therapist decided that it was not necessary to recommend disclosure. However, the therapist strongly

suggested to the husband that in the future he work to resolve his differences with his wife rather than do something without her knowledge that she opposed.

(3) A 10-year-old boy, whose parents were divorced, revealed that the last time he was at his father's house he and his father had gotten into an argument and his father had called him a name. He didn't want his mother to know about this incident because he was afraid she would overreact and try to prevent him from spending time with his father. The boy didn't object to the therapist discussing the incident with his father and with him and his father together. The therapist decided that this was sufficient and did not recommend disclosure to mother.

(4) A 15-year-old boy revealed that when he was in elementary school he had regularly gone to a local store to shoplift candy bars and comic books. He stopped this behavior when he entered junior high school and had not engaged in it since. He was feeling guilty and ashamed about the shoplifting and didn't want his parents to know about it. The therapist decided that it was not necessary for him to recommend disclosure because the shoplifting behavior had stopped and there was no evidence that the boy was feeling any urge to resume it.

## The Patient's Confidentiality

In addition to discussing the therapist's position on confidentiality, it is also important to discuss recommendations to family members about their own confidentiality. Generally, the most effective strategy is to tell individuals that it is up to them whether or not they discuss their individual interviews with other family members and vice versa. However, it is important to also say that if they ever were to hear about something from another family member that the therapist reportedly said in an individual interview that might be upsetting to them, they should discuss it with the therapist. For example, one husband told his wife that in his individual interview the therapist had said, "You have problems in your marriage because your wife can't control her anger." In fact, what the therapist had said was, "Yes, I agree with you that your wife's anger is one of the reasons that the two of you have trouble getting along with each other." Clarification of this issue with both the wife and the husband was essential in order for the therapy to proceed effectively.

## INTEGRATION OF CONJOINT AND INDIVIDUAL ASSESSMENT INTERVIEWS

Integration of conjoint and individual assessment interviews allows the therapist to utilize the specific benefits of each interview context. With families, the assessment process consists of one or more interviews with the parents, one or more interviews with the symptomatic child or adolescent, and one or more conjoint family interviews. With couples, there are one or more conjoint interviews with the couple and one or more individual interviews with each partner. In the folling section, a method for integrating these different interview formats will be described.

## Families

### Interview With Parents

The initial interview with the parents provides the therapist with an opportunity to gather detailed information about the presenting problems, to place these problems in perspective by collecting information about the family history, to discuss the parents' current and past attempts at problem solution, and to explore individual and familial strengths. It also allows the therapist to observe the parents' interactional patterns with each other and with the therapist. The process of establishing a positive working alliance with the parents begins here.

When the parents are married and living together, the initial interview is a conjoint interview with both parents. When they are separated or divorced, it is generally best, at least initially, to meet individually with each parent. In either case, it is essential to involve *both* parents in the assessment process. Each parent's perceptions of the problems and strengths of the symptomatic child or adolescent and of the family are of the utmost importance. Areas of disagreement between the parents' perceptions are also of great importance, as is the process used by the parents to discuss these differences. By observing the parents' interactions as they discuss their different perceptions, the therapist learns a great deal about the structure and functioning of the family system.

It is essential to involve both parents in the assessment process because this process is the foundation for therapeutic intervention. Effective therapeutic work with children and/or adolescents and their families requires a strong and balanced working alliance between the therapist and both parents. When one parent is excluded from the initial assessment, the therapist's ability to create such an alliance is severely handicapped.

Initially, it is helpful to ask each parent to write down what he or she considers to be the major problems and strengths in the family (Feldman, 1985b) and to complete a comprehensive symptom checklist (e.g., Achenbach, 1981) in regard to the symptomatic child or adolescent. These written materials provide the therapist with a great deal of clinically useful information. They also provide an initial baseline for evaluating progress in therapy.

If the parents have brought evaluations or notes from other sources (teachers, probation officers, etc.), the therapist reads them and requests copies for his or her records. In many instances, the therapist also seeks permission from the parents (and, in the individual interview, from the child or adolescent) to contact these important extrafamilial adults directly. Information obtained from these contacts is often of great diagnostic and therapeutic significance.

At the beginning of the verbal interview, it is helpful to ask the parents if they have any questions for the therapist. Parents are generally appreciative of the opportunity to ask such questions, even if they do not follow through on the opportunity at that time. When parents do ask questions, usually they ask about one of three issues: (1) the therapist's training and experience; (2) the therapist's orientation and approach; or (3) the therapist's experience or lack of experience as a parent. These questions are best answered in a straightforward way, without interpretation or judgment.

Initially, the therapist explains his or her position on confidentiality, answering any questions that the parents may have about this issue. Then, he or she begins a detailed assessment of the presenting problems. The therapist helps the parents to transform vague, general problem statements—such as, "He's impossible"; "She's afraid of everything"—into clear, specific problem identifications—such as, "He doesn't do what I ask him to do most of the time and about half the time when I ask him to do something he yells and curses at me"; "She says she is afraid to go to school but doesn't know why. She also says she is afraid to go to sleep at night because she might have bad dreams."

The nature, intensity, frequency, and duration of each presenting problem are explored and clarified, as are the circumstances within which the problems generally arise. Particular attention is directed toward the identification of family interactional patterns that are associated with the onset or exacerbation of symptomatic behaviors or emotions.

In addition to the problems of the identified patient, the therapist also asks about problems with other family members (e.g., siblings, parents, grandparents) and problems in the parents' marriage. If problems with one or more other family members or with the marriage are identified, these are thoroughly discussed.

Once the presenting problems have been identified, the history of each problem is delineated. The objective is to obtain a clear understanding of when and how each of the problems first appeared; the course of problem development over time; and the nature of any events that were associated with problem development or exacerbation—such as, births, deaths, illnesses, separations. If there are any indications of intrafamilial or extrafamilial abuse (verbal, physical, or sexual), these are thoroughly investigated.

The therapist then focuses on the parents' past and current responses to their child's symptomatic behavior. Each parent's usual ways of responding are explored, and constructive and nonconstructive responses are identified. The therapist also identifies any inconsistencies or conflicts between the parents. Not uncommonly, parents are overtly or covertly at odds with each other about how best to deal with their child's problematic behavior. It is important to identify and clarify such differences, and it is also important to carefully observe the interactional process between the parents as they discuss their differences.

If there have been any previous evaluations or therapies, the parents are asked about their reactions to these experiences. If their reactions were primarily positive, the therapist clarifies what they felt positive about. If their reactions were primarily negative, the therapist explores what led to the negative feelings. By having this information, the therapist is in a position to avoid pitfalls that may have limited the effectiveness of previous therapies and to make use of strategies that have previously been helpful.

A detailed exploration of the reasons for seeking help at this particular time is essential. Did the initiative for seeking help come from the parents, the school, the legal system, or the symptomatic child or adolescent? What was the sequence of events leading up to the decision to seek help? What are the parents' expectations of the assessment? What kind of help do they want? All of these questions need to be explored, as well as an explanation given about what can realistically be expected from the assessment process.

When the problems have been thoroughly discussed, the focus is shifted from problems to strengths. The parents are asked to identify areas of positive individual and family functioning—for example, "What is there about your son's behavior that you are feeling good about?"; "What are his strengths?"; "What do you like about the way things are currently going in the family?"

In addition to asking about present strengths, the therapist also asks about strengths that were present in the past but are not currently in evidence—for example, "What were things like in the family before these problems developed?"; "What have been your daughter's strengths in the past?"; "What did you like about the way she was at that time?"

A developmental history of the family and of the symptomatic child or adolescent is of great importance. Developmental delays or difficulties are explored, along with any familial stresses that may have been associated with these developmental problems.

The final step in the initial interview with the parents is planning for the individual meeting with the symptomatic child or adolescent. At this point, the therapist and parents discuss how much, if any, of what the parents have said about their child or adolescent the therapist may wish to share with him or her and how much, if any, of what the child or adolescent says in his or her interview will be shared with the parents. The therapist also discusses with the parents what they have told the child or adolescent about why he or she is coming for an interview. If nothing has yet been said to the youngster, the therapist asks the parents what they were thinking of saying. If the therapist agrees with their ideas, he or she affirms them. If the therapist does not agree, an alternative approach is suggested. Generally, the best strategy is to suggest a simple, straightforward statement like "We want you to meet with someone who helps children with problems like the ones you've been having lately" (Cohen, 1979).

*Interview With Symptomatic Child or Adolescent*

The initial individual interview with the symptomatic child or adolescent is directed toward an exploration of the young person's feelings and thoughts about the presenting problems, about himself or herself, and about his or her family. With adolescents, generally the interview is entirely verbal. With younger children, verbal interviewing is combined with diagnostic play activities, such as picture drawing, story telling, doll and puppet play, and therapeutic board games (Broder & Hood, 1983; Gardner, 1979; Greenspan, 1981; E. Wachtel, 1987).

As with the parents, it is helpful initially to ask the child or adolescent to write down what he or she considers to be the major problems and strengths in the family (Feldman, 1985b). Older children and adolescents are also asked to complete a comprehensive symptom checklist (e.g., Achenbach & Edelbrock, 1981) in regard to themselves. The information derived from these instruments provides a helpful overview of the young person's experience of self and family. It also provides an initial baseline for evaluating progress in therapy.

When the written materials have been completed, the therapist asks the youngster to accompany him or her to the meeting room. Usually this is a smooth transition. Sometimes, however, especially with younger children, there may be a great deal of separation anxiety and consequent resistance to coming with the therapist. When this is the case, a few minutes of relaxed conversation in the waiting room are usually sufficient to reduce the anxiety and overcome the resistance. When this is not sufficient, the best strategy is to invite the parents to accompany the child to the interview room and to stay for the first part of the interview. Most anxious children are able to tolerate separation from their parents at some point during the interview. For those who are not, the entire interview is conducted with the parents present. In these instances, a second individual interview is scheduled, with the hope that separation will be more tolerable at that time.

At the beginning of the individual interview, the therapist explains his or her position on confidentiality and answers any questions that the child or adolescent may have about this issue. Then, the therapist asks the young person about his or her understanding of the reasons for the consultation (e.g., "What have you been told about why you are coming for this meeting?") and about his or her feelings about being there. Discussion of these issues at the beginning facilitates the development of rapport and helps to focus the interview on those problems that are of most concern to the child or adolescent.

In discussing problems, the therapist's questions are primarily directed toward an exploration of the young person's feelings and thoughts, for example, "When you have trouble going to sleep at night, what feelings are you usually having?"; "What do you usually think about during those times?"; "Have you been feeling sad lately?"; "Did you get mad when he said that?" The number and wording of such questions need to be congruent with the child or adolescent's age, developmental level, and attentional, perceptual, and cognitive abilities.

The therapist inquires about problems in the family, at school, and with peers. The history and development of each problem are delineated, and current circumstances associated with the onset or exacerbation of problems are explored. Attention is also directed toward the young person's perception of his or her parents' usual reactions to the emergence or escalation of problems and his or her feelings and thoughts about those reactions.

In addition to identifying problems, the therapist also identifies strengths. What aspects of his or her life is the young person feeling good about? What does he or she see as personal strengths? What does he or she view as the positive aspects of his or her family? Focusing on the positives as well as the negatives helps to develop a more balanced perspective, to counter demoralization, and to foster the creation of a hopeful, change-promoting atmosphere.

With adolescents and older children, a personal and family history is taken. This history is directed toward clarification of the developmental course of the presenting problems, the young person's efforts to cope with those problems, the parents' efforts to cope with the problems, and positive aspects of individual and family functioning that were present in the past but are currently being inhibited or blocked.

With younger children, diagnostic play activities are an important part of the initial interview. This may be either unstructured or structured. In an unstructured play interview (Greenspan, 1981), a variety of play materials are made available and the child is told that he or she may play with any of them. The therapist is primarily an observer of the child's play, although he or she may ask an occasional question or make an occasional comment about the play (e.g., "What is the daddy bear feeling?"; "The boy in that picture looks sad").

In a more structured play interview, the therapist picks a few specific play activities and invites the child to participate in them one at a time. For some activities, the therapist observes, asks questions, or makes comments. For others, he or she is a more active participant. For example, in using Gardner's "Talking, Feeling, and Doing Game" (1979), both child and therapist answer questions about their feelings, thoughts, and behaviors. The therapist's responses are designed to foster the development of rapport, to serve as a model for emotional expression, and to explore hypotheses about the child's feelings and conflicts.

Unstructured and structured play interviews each have advantages and limitations. With an unstructured interview, the therapist can observe the pattern of the child's spontaneous behavior over time, including shifts from one activity to another. With a more structured interview, specific diagnostic information can often be obtained more quickly and efficiently. Usually, the most helpful approach is to use a combination of unstructured and structured play.

Shortly before the end of the interview, it is helpful to mention to the young person that it is almost time to stop. This makes for a gradual rather than sudden transition, providing an opportunity for the child to finish whatever activity he or she has been involved with.

Throughout the course of the interview, the therapist carefully observes the young person's nonverbal and verbal behavior, noting any abnormalities of gait, coordination, movement (tics, tremors, hyperactivity, etc.), speech, attention, or emotional expression (anxiety, depression, aggression, etc.). The therapist also notes behavioral and emotional strengths, aptitudes, and interests (Cohen, 1979).

### Conjoint Family Interview

The third major component of an integrative multilevel assessment with families is a conjoint family interview. This interview always includes the parents and the symptomatic child or adolescent. It may also include other family members (e.g., siblings, grandparents) if the therapist believes their presence is necessary for a comprehensive assessment.

When the parents are married and living together, they both participate in the same conjoint interview. When the parents are separated or divorced, it is usually best, at least initially, to conduct separate conjoint interviews with each parent.

At the beginning of the conjoint family interview, each family member is asked to think about how things are presently going in the family and to identify one aspect of family life that he or she is feeling good about and would like to continue just as it is. Family members are then asked to share their thoughts and feelings with each other. Focusing initially on positive feelings fosters the creation of a collaborative and cooperative climate. This climate facilitates subsequent discussions of individual and interactional problems.

After the discussion of positive behaviors, family members are asked to identify one aspect of family life that they wish would be different. They are then asked to discuss their thoughts and feelings and to attempt to reach one or more mutually acceptable behavior-change agreements.

One goal of this procedure is to observe the family's communication and problem-solving process and their responses to feedback from the therapist about this process. When the therapist observes a dysfunctional behavior pattern (e.g., vague, generalized statements; lack of focus on a single issue at a time; interruptions; verbal abuse), he or she comments on this pattern and makes suggestions about a more constructive alternative. Examples of such suggestions are "Mrs. Jones, what exactly would you like Johnny to be doing differently?"; "Folks, let's deal with one issue at a time"; "Susan, I know you're angry with your parents, but I would like you to find another way of expressing your anger that does not involve calling them names."

The therapist clarifies family members' requests for change and helps them to express these requests in clear, specific language. Examples of such requests are "Mom, I would like you to stop lecturing me about what I should be doing differently in school"; "Sarah, we want you to come home by curfew every time you go out"; "Dad, I wish you would stop yelling at me"; "Billy, I want you to stop calling me names and kicking me when you get angry."

The therapist also helps family members identify and communicate the emotional reactions that have led to their requests. Examples of such communications are "Mom, when you lecture me like that I feel like a moron"; "Sarah, when you don't come home by curfew, we get very worried"; "Dad, when you yell at me I feel like you hate me"; "Billy, calling me names hurts me a great deal."

After each family member has made at least one request for change by one or more of the other family members, attention is turned to each person's feelings and thoughts about the requests that have been made of him or her. The therapist helps family members identify positive and negative reactions to the requested changes and then facilitates discussion of these reactions. In the course of this discussion, some changes in or additions to the original request may be made. Often, a counterrequest is made by the person on the receiving end of the original request, for example, "Mom, the reason I call you names is that you won't stop telling me what to do"; "Son, the reason I yell at you is because you don't answer me when I talk to you." The therapist helps family members negotiate their differences in such a way that one or more initial behavior-change agreements can be reached.

## Formulation and Treatment Plan

By integrating the information and observations derived from the interviews with the parents, child or adolescent, and family, the therapist is in a position to develop a comprehensive diagnostic formulation. This formulation includes an assessment of the nature and intensity of individual and family problems, the intrapsychic and interpersonal processes that are stimulating and reinforcing these problems, and the individual and familial strengths that are limiting the severity of the problems and providing a foundation for constructive problem resolution.

On the basis of the diagnostic formulation, the therapist develops recommendations for therapy. These recommendations are then discussed, individually and conjointly, with the parents and the symptomatic child or adolescent. The therapist explains his or her rationale for the particular treatment plan being recommended, asking for feedback from family members about this recommendation. Based on the feedback, the recommended treatment plan may be accepted, or one or more modifications may be introduced. In either case, it is best to implement the agreed-upon treatment plan on a time-limited basis (e.g., one month) and then reassess whether to retain or modify the existing plan.

## Couples

With couples, the assessment process consists of one or more conjoint interviews with the couple and one or more individual interviews with each partner. As with families, it is helpful initially to have each partner write down what he or she considers to be the major problems and strengths in their family (Feldman, 1985b) and to complete a comprehensive symptom checklist in regard to him- or herself (e.g., the SCL-90, Lipman, Covi, & Shapiro, 1977). These forms are briefly reviewed with each partner individually prior to the beginning of the initial conjoint interview.

### Conjoint Interview

The initial conjoint interview with a couple begins in the same way as the initial interview with the parents of a symptomatic child or adolescent—that is, the therapist asks if either spouse would like to ask any questions. Generally, if there are questions, they relate to the therapist's training and experience, therapeutic approach, or marital status. As previously noted, such questions are best answered in a straightforward manner, without interpretation or judgment.

The therapist's first questions to the couple are directed toward delineation and clarification of the presenting problems. Each partner is asked to identify what he or she considers to be the major problems at the present time. The therapist helps the couple to transform vague, general statements—for example, "Lack of communication"; "Too much conflict"; "Bob's depression"; "Mary's complaining" —into clear, specific problem identifications—for example, "We very seldom (less than once a week) talk with each other about our feelings"; "We argue almost every day. Usually these are verbal arguments, but three or four times a year they become physical fights"; "Bob spends most of each morning sleeping and then mopes around the house the rest of the day"; "Mary complains that I work too many hours, but she also complains that I don't make enough money."

The therapist then helps the partners express their emotional reactions to the identified problems—for example, "When he doesn't want to talk with me, I feel hurt and rejected"; "I hate arguing; I feel awful while the argument is happening and I feel even worse after it's over"; "I'm worried about Bob, but I'm also angry with him because he refuses to take medication for his depression"; "I feel like I can't win with Mary. No matter what I do it's never good enough for her."

After discussing each person's perceptions of the major problems and the emotional reactions to those problems, the history of each problem is delineated. Particular attention is directed toward (1) events associated with problem development, exacerbation, or improvement (e.g., one or both partners starting or ending a career, the birth of a child, the death of a parent); (2) the couple's attempts at problem solution (including any previous or current psychotherapy or pharmacotherapy); and (3) the specific reasons for seeking help at this time.

In exploring the couple's attempts at problem solution, the therapist focuses on behaviors that have met with some measure of success as well as those that have either failed to solve the problems or made them worse. If there have been any previous therapies, each person's feelings about those experiences are discussed and the specific reasons for positive or negative reactions are clarified.

It is important to discuss the reasons why help is being sought at this particular time. When was the idea of coming for help first discussed? Who initiated the discussion? What was the other person's reaction? What was the sequence of events that led to the decision to come for help? What kind of help is each person seeking (e.g., marital therapy or divorce therapy; help for self, partner, or the relationship)?

After the problems have been identified and their histories explored, the spouses are asked to translate problem statements into requests for behavioral change and to present these requests directly to each other. The person on the receiving end of a request is asked to listen carefully and to monitor his or her positive and negative reactions to the request. These reactions are then communicated to the other and an attempt is made to negotiate at least one behavior-change agreement. During this process, the therapist observes the couple's problem-solving efforts, identifies dysfunctional interactions, and suggests more constructive alternatives—for example, "Bob, please look at Mary when you talk to her"; "Mary, instead of telling Bob that he's hopeless, please tell him exactly what he's doing that is upsetting you"; "I would like you both to stop talking for a moment and just think about what the other person has been saying."

Following the problem-solving discussion, the focus is shifted from problems to strengths. Each partner is asked to specify those aspects of the relationship that he or she has positive feelings about (e.g., "What is there about how things are presently going in your relationship that you are feeling good about?") and those aspects of the other's behavior that are pleasing (e.g., "What does he do that you like?"). In addition to inquiring about present strengths, the therapist also asks about strengths in the past (e.g., "Was there a time when you both were feeling good about your relationship? What were things like back then?").

A brief history of the relationship is then taken, starting with the couple's first meeting and tracing the development of the relationship to the present time. One purpose of this history is to help clarify the development of the presenting problems. A second, and equally important, purpose is to focus attention on positive aspects of the relationship that have been present in the past but are currently being suppressed by negative interactions and emotions.

At the end of the initial conjoint interview, the therapist summarizes his or her understanding of each partner's thoughts and feelings about the problems and strengths in their relationship and clarifies any aspects of this summary that either partner perceives as unclear, inaccurate, or incomplete. Then, the therapist explains that the next step in the assessment process will be an individual interview with each partner, giving a brief rationale for these interviews. Generally, the best explanation is that by meeting with the partners individually as well as together the therapist will be able to develop a more complete understanding of their relationship and of each person's feelings and thoughts about the relationship and about him- or herself.

## Individual Interviews

Individual assessment interviews are conducted with each partner. Structurally, it is helpful to conduct these individual interviews back-to-back. This allows the therapist to maintain a connection with the couple as a couple while beginning to develop an individual relationship with each partner. Individual interviews should be scheduled as close together as possible on the same day if back-to-back scheduling is not possible.

The therapist begins with an explanation of his or her position on confidentiality, answering any questions that may arise in regard to this issue. Then, he or she inquires about how things are currently going and how things have been since the initial conjoint interview. As the therapist listens to each spouse's responses to these questions, his or her attention is directed toward clarification and elaboration of each partner's feelings and thoughts about the presenting problems, the relationship, the other partner, and the self.

At first, the focus is on the individual's own feelings (e.g., "When Sue comes home late, what feelings do you start to feel?"; "When you get angry, are you aware of also feeling hurt?"). Later, the therapist shifts the focus to the other's subjective experience (e.g., "What are the things Sue gets angry about?"; "What is your understanding of what she is asking you to do differently? Why is that important to her?").

When there has been some degree of emotional clarification, the therapist focuses on the cognitive processes that underlie the experienced emotions. For example: "When you first started to feel angry, what thoughts were you thinking?"; "What goes through your mind when you start to feel sad?"; "When he does that, what words do you say to yourself? What feelings do those words lead to?" Discussion of the nature and importance of automatic thoughts is helpful, along with discussion of specific techniques for monitoring such thoughts during the course of day-to-day interaction (Beck, 1976).

In addition to discussing the problems, it is equally important to discuss individual and relational strengths.

Which aspects of the relationship is each person feeling good about? What behaviors of the other are pleasing to him or her? What elements of his or her own behavior are sources of satisfaction and pride? What does each partner wish to continue unchanged about the other, him- or herself, and the relationship? After discussing present strengths, the therapist asks about past strengths—for example, "What attracted you to him or her?"; "What were things like at the beginning of your relationship?"; "What did you enjoy about being with him or her back then?"

When the problems and strengths have been sufficiently clarified, the therapist shifts to an exploration of the history of each family of origin. This provides a foundation for developing an understanding of the connections between feelings, thoughts, and behaviors in relation to the partner and conscious or unconscious feelings and thoughts in relation to members of the family of origin (i.e., transference reactions). Each partner's feelings and thoughts about his or her relationship with each parent and sibling are thoroughly discussed, along with any other family relationships that were of particular importance (e.g., with grandparents, aunts, uncles, cousins).

## Formulation and Treatment Plan

The information and observations derived from the conjoint and individual interviews are utilized to develop a comprehensive diagnostic formulation. This formulation includes an assessment of the nature and intensity of individual and relationship problems, the interpersonal and intrapsychic factors that are stimulating and reinforcing these problems, and the individual and interpersonal strengths that are limiting the severity of the problems and are providing a foundation for constructive problem resolution.

Based on the diagnostic formulation, the therapist generates recommendations for therapy. These recommendations are then discussed with the couple in a conjoint interview. During the course of this discussion, the original recommendations may be accepted, or one or more modifications may be introduced. In either case, when a treatment plan has been agreed to, it is implemented on a time-limited basis (e.g., one month) and then reassessed.

# 3

*Integrative Multilevel
Treatment Planning*

INTEGRATIVE MULTILEVEL treatment planning is directed toward the development of a comprehensive, multilevel therapeutic structure. This structure is designed to promote a decrease in individual and family interactional problems and an increase in individual and family interactional strengths. The first step in the development of such a structure is clarification of each family member's explicit and implicit therapeutic goals.

## GOALS

When individuals or families come for psychotherapy, they come for a reason; they want something to be different. The therapist needs to identify what each family member wants to be different about him- or herself, other family members, and the family as a whole.

In general, family members' goals can be grouped into two major categories: (1) desired decreases in the frequency and/or intensity of unpleasant or dysfunctional emotions, cognitions, or behaviors; and (2) desired increases in the frequency and/or intensity of pleasant or functional emotions, cognitions, or behaviors. Both types of goals are equally important and each should receive an equal degree of the therapist's attention.

Often, different family members identify different, and sometimes conflicting, goals. For example: (1) The parents of a depressed adolescent boy identified their major goal for the therapy as the alleviation of their son's depression; the boy indicated that his major goal was a reduction in the level of conflict between him and his parents; (2) A husband stated that his goal in coming for marital therapy was to improve his marriage; the wife stated that her goal was to dissolve the marriage.

Differences in family members' therapeutic goals often emerge only during individual interviews. Therefore, it is essential that both individual and conjoint interviews be utilized during the process of goal clarification. When the therapist is aware that different family members have different therapeutic goals, he or she can help them negotiate a therapeutic contract that takes into account each of their desired objectives. Establishment of a viable therapeutic contract is very difficult if the therapist is not aware of these differences. Under those conditions, whatever treatment plan is agreed to is likely to be undermined by the therapist's ignorance of the differences between different family members' goals.

When the therapist discovers that two or more family members have conflicting therapeutic goals, he or she utilizes individual and conjoint interviews to explore the possibility of developing a set of treatment goals that, at least temporarily, are acceptable to all family members. In doing this, the notion of time-limited goals is often very helpful. For example, a couple comes for marital therapy and the wife reveals in an individual interview that she is uncertain about whether she wants to stay in the marriage. The therapist can explore the wife's feelings and determine whether she is willing to make a time-limited commitment to try to improve the marriage, reevaluating her feelings at the end of that time period. If she is willing to make such a commitment, then marital therapy is possible. Divorce therapy is the only possible option if the wife is not willing to make such a commitment.

## STRUCTURE

After exploring each family member's therapeutic goals, the therapist recommends a treatment structure that he or she believes is most likely to work toward the attainment of those goals. This structure involves either symmetrical or asymmetrical integration of individual and family interviews.

Both individual and family interviews are uniquely valuable contexts for therapeutic intervention. Each format has specific strengths and limitations. Integration of these formats allows the therapist to draw upon the strengths of each, to design therapeutic structures that meet the specific needs of particular individuals and families, and to flexibly alter the therapy structure in response to changing individual or family interactional dynamics.

Conjoint family and family subgroup interviews are particularly valuable contexts for promoting interpersonal changes because they allow the therapist to give direct and immediate feedback to family members in response to functional and dysfunctional interactions, to suggest and/or model positive interactional changes, and to help families practice new ways of interacting in a safe, supervised setting. Conjoint interviews are also valuable sources of hypotheses about intrapsychic factors that may be contributing to dysfunctional family interactional patterns. These hypotheses are helpful guides to the generation of therapeutic interventions to alter the dysfunctional interactions.

Individual interviews are particularly valuable contexts for promoting individual changes because they facilitate intensive discussion of conscious and preconscious feelings and thoughts, they lower resistance to self-exploration and self-modification, and they provide an opportunity for individuals to practice behavioral changes with the therapist prior to trying them out in the family. Individual interviews are also valuable sources of hypotheses about interpersonal factors that may be contributing to dysfunctional intrapsychic reaction patterns. These hypotheses are helpful guides to generating therapeutic interventions to alter the dysfunctional intrapsychic reactions.

Conjoint and individual interviews can be integrated in either a symmetrical or an asymmetrical structure. Table 3.1 provides an overview of the different forms that such a structural integration may take.

**TABLE 3.1**

INTEGRATING INDIVIDUAL AND FAMILY INTERVIEWS

| TYPE OF INTEGRATION | CHARCTERISTICS |
| --- | --- |
| *Symmetrical* | Equal use of individual and family interviews |
| *Asymmetrical* | |
|   Individually oriented | Individual interviews used more than family interviews |
|   Family-oriented | Family interviews used more than individual interviews |
| *Sequential* | Individual and family interviews used on different visits |
| *Combined* | Individual and family interviews used during the same visit |

## Symmetrical or Asymmetrical Integration

*Symmetrical integration* is characterized by an equal emphasis on each type of interview format. In symmetrical therapy with couples, conjoint interviews with the couple alternate with concurrent individual interviews with each partner. In symmetrical therapy with families, conjoint interviews with the family or a family subgroup (e.g., parents) alternate with individual interviews with the symptomatic child or adolescent.

With both couples and families, conjoint and individual interviews can either take place on separate visits or each visit can be divided into conjoint and individual components. For instance, a conjoint family interview can be followed by an individual interview with the symptomatic child or adolescent; individual interviews with each member of a couple can be followed by a conjoint interview with the couple.

*Asymmetrical integration* is characterized by an emphasis on one interview format more than the other. In asymmetrical therapy with couples, the structure is either (1) two or more conjoint interviews in a row followed by one set of individual interviews (conjoint-oriented integration); or (2) two or more sets of individual interviews followed by one conjoint interview (individually oriented integration). In asymmetrical therapy with families, the structure is either (1) two or more conjoint interviews with the family or family subgroup followed by one individual interview with the symptomatic child or adolescent (conjoint-oriented integration); or (2) two or more individual interviews with the child or adolescent followed by one conjoint interview with the family or family subgroup (individually oriented integration).

As with symmetrical integration, the conjoint and individual interviews may take place on different visits or each visit may be divided into asymmetrical components; for example, 15 minutes with the family followed by a 45-minute individual interview with the child or adolescent; 15 minutes with each member of a couple followed by a 45-minute conjoint couple interview.

Table 3.2 presents an overview of the indications for symmetrical and asymmetrical integration. Generally, a symmetrical structure is indicated when the level of individual and family interactional dysfunction is equally high. When there is a higher level of individual dysfunction than of family interactional dysfunction, an individually oriented

**TABLE 3.2**
INDICATIONS FOR SYMMETRICAL AND
ASYMMETRICAL INTEGRATION

| TYPE OF INTEGRATION | INDICATIONS |
|---|---|
| *Symmetrical* | Equally high degree of individual and family dysfunction |
| | No major resistance to either individual or family interviews |
| *Asymmetrical* Individually oriented | Higher degree of individual than family dysfunction |
| | and/or |
| | Major resistance to family interviews |
| Family-oriented | Higher degree of family than individual dysfunction |
| | and/or |
| | Major resistance to individual interviews |
| *Sequential* | Consructive use of both individual and family interviews |
| *Combined* | Blocks to construcive use of either individual or family interviews |
| | and/or |
| | Termination phase of therapy |

integration is indicated. A family-oriented structure is indicated when there is a higher level of family interactional dysfunction than of individual dysfunction.

In addition to assessing the level of individual and family interactional dysfunction, the therapist also assesses the level of resistance to individual and conjoint interviews. When there is a high degree of resistance to one of the formats, it is usually best to begin with an asymmetrical structure, with the primary emphasis on the least resisted format. Later in the therapy it may be possible to make an adjustment if the therapist believes a more symmetrical structure would be most helpful.

Combining individual and family interviews during the same visit is often helpful when family members have difficulty making good use of one of the interview formats. For example, a highly conflictual couple may have great difficulty engaging in constructive problem solving during a conjoint interview unless it is preceded by individual interviews in which each spouse can ventilate some of his or her hostility as preparation to listen to the other's point of view. Conversely, a child may have difficulty engaging in an individual interview unless it is preceded by a conjoint family interview in which individual and family interactional problems and strengths are identified and discussed.

The combined format is also useful during the termination phase of therapy, when the frequency of visits is typically reduced. For example, when conjoint family interviews have been alternating with individual child interviews on a once-a-week schedule, it is often helpful to combine the two formats when the frequency is reduced to once every two weeks.

The recommended frequency of therapy meetings is determined primarily by the severity of the presenting problems. When the severity of the problems is great (e.g., acute suicidal crisis, marital or parent-child violence, severe agoraphobia, school avoidance), the frequency of therapy should be high—for example, two or three times per week. When the problems are less severe, once a week is usually sufficient. Over time, the frequency of therapy meetings can be decreased or increased in response to changes in the severity of the problems.

The duration of therapy is determined by the severity of the presenting problems, the degree of individual and familial motivation for change, and the nature of the therapeutic objectives. When the problems are of relatively moderate severity, when family members are highly motivated to change, and when therapeutic goals are relatively modest, the length of therapy may be brief (1–6 months). With more severe problems, with less motivated individuals and families, and with more ambitious therapeutic objectives, the duration of therapy is usually longer (6 months to 1 or more years).

In most instances, individual and family therapy integration can be effectively conducted by a single therapist. Indeed, there are specific advantages to a one-therapist structure: (1) the therapist has direct access to the information and observations derived from the individual and family interviews; (2) the therapist has the opportunity to form both individual and conjoint therapeutic alliances; (3) there is maximum coordination of the individual and family therapy components; (4) there is maximum flexibility in regard to structure change (i.e., increasing or decreasing the frequency or length of individual or conjoint interviews); and (5) there is minimum conflict between the individual and family therapists.

There are times, however, when it is better to divide the work between two therapists. When this is done with families, one therapist meets with the symptomatic child or adolescent, the other therapist meets with the parents, and both therapists meet with the family. With couples, a different therapist meets individually with each of the spouses and both therapists meet with the couple. Such a "collaborative" structure is indicated when the number and/or severity of individual and family problems is unusually high or when one family member is unusually resistant to sharing "his or her" therapist with the other family members.

The structure of the therapy is arrived at by a process of collaboration between the therapist and family. During the assessment process, the therapist elicits each family member's reactions to the conjoint and individual interviews. These reactions are then combined with the therapist's perceptions of the therapeutic needs of the family and its individual members, leading to a recommendation for either a symmetrical or asymmetrical therapy structure. This recommendation is then discussed with the family members and an agreed-upon structure is arrived at.

When a therapeutic structure has been agreed to, it is best to implement it initially on a time-limited basis (e.g., one month). After that period, the therapist and family can reassess the structure of the therapy, either retaining the existing structure or changing it if it appears that the therapy would proceed more effectively with a different structure. Subsequently, the structure may remain the same or it may be changed one or more times based on the therapist's and family's ongoing assessment of individual and family-system needs and resistances.

## Clinical Illustrations

### Couples—Symmetrical Integration

Alan and Carol, a couple in their late 30s, came for marital therapy because of dysfunctional conflict and lack of intimacy in their marriage. The immediate precipitant of their request for help was a recent argument in which Alan had grabbed Carol and pushed her into a chair. This was the first time that either of them had ever been physically violent during their 10-year marriage, although each had been verbally abusive toward the other on many occasions.

In the initial conjoint interview, Alan and Carol were both very anxious and somewhat depressed as they recounted the events leading up to their decision to seek therapy. They were guarded in their exchanges with each other and, at times, were verbally hostile. They both expressed a good deal of confusion, frustration, and sadness about the lack of verbal or physical intimacy in their relationship. Both also expressed a strong desire to preserve their marriage, if positive changes could be made.

In their individual interviews, Alan and Carol elaborated on their feelings about each other, their marriage, and themselves. Alan indicated that he often felt criticized and demeaned by Carol and that when he felt himself to be "under attack," he became enraged. He typically expressed this rage by yelling at Carol, although he sometimes felt an urge to be physically aggressive toward her. During the most recent conflict, he lost control of this urge and pushed her down. He felt guilty, ashamed, and remorseful about this behavior; he wanted help so that it would not be repeated. At the same time, he wanted Carol to get help so that she would be less demeaning and more affirming of him.

Carol indicated that she often felt neglected by Alan, which was extremely frustrating and hurtful to her. The argument that led to their seeking therapy occurred shortly after Alan had returned from one of his frequent business trips. Carol had been hoping that they would spend an intimate evening together focused on their relationship. Instead, Alan talked at great length about the details of his business trip. After awhile, Carol began making sarcastic remarks about Alan and his business. He became enraged and called her a "bitch." She responded with an equally insulting remark, and the argument began to escalate. Eventually, Alan shoved Carol into a chair. They were both shocked and disheartened by this behavior and realized that they needed therapeutic help.

Interpersonal and intrapsychic factors appeared to be making an equal contribution to Alan and Carol's problems. At the interpersonal level, their communication and problem-solving skills were severely underdeveloped. They were not able to express their feelings clearly and constructively, they were not able to actively and empathically listen to each other, and they were not able to negotiate mutually acceptable behavior-change agreements.

At the intrapsychic level, Alan and Carol's problems were derived from each person's cognitive distortions (magnification of the other's negative behaviors, minimization of one's own negative behaviors and of the other's positive behaviors, overgeneralization, arbitrary inference); unrealistic expectations (Alan unconsciously expected Carol to be totally admiring; Carol unconsciously expected Alan to be totally attentive); and narcissistic vulnerabilities (Alan was unconsciously afraid of being engulfed by Carol; Carol was unconsciously afraid of being abandoned by Alan).

Since Alan and Carol had each responded positively to both the conjoint and individual interviews, a symmetrical therapeutic structure was recommended. One week the spouses were seen conjointly; the next week they were each seen individually. In the conjoint interviews, they worked primarily on developing more clear and empathic communication and more constructive and effective problem-solving interactions. In the individual interviews, each spouse worked on identifying and countering dysfunctional cognitions, experiencing and reducing irrational anxieties and conflicts, and practicing new forms of interactional behavior.

The symmetrical structure worked well for Alan and Carol; therefore it was maintained during the course of their 10-month therapy. When they terminated, the frequency and intensity of dysfunctional conflicts had greatly diminished and the frequency and intensity of positive intimacy had increased.

*Couples—Asymmetrical Integration*

*Conjoint-oriented.* Emily and Dan had been married for five years when they came for marital therapy. Their presenting problem was sexual dysfunction. Emily was nonorgasmic; Dan ejaculated prematurely. These problems were a source of frustration and anxiety for both of them. Lately, they had been avoiding sex altogether.

In other areas of their relationship, Emily and Dan both reported primarily positive feelings. They enjoyed spending time together and shared many interests in common. However, their sexual problems were starting to erode the overall positive tone of their relationship.

In their initial individual interviews, Emily and Dan both expressed a good deal of anxiety and frustration about their sexual problems but also expressed many positive feelings about the other and about their relationship. Each described his or her family of origin as generally nurturing and supportive, without major traumatic disruptions or conflicts.

Since the major dysfunction in Emily and Dan's relationship appeared to be interactional, a conjoint-oriented therapy structure was recommended. They came for conjoint interviews once a week for three weeks, then came for one set of concurrent individual interviews, then another three weeks of conjoint interviews, and so forth. In the conjoint interviews, the focus was on the interactional aspects of their sexual relationship. Sensate focus exercises and other behavioral sex therapy techniques were utilized as the primary therapeutic interventions. In the individual interviews, their feelings and thoughts about their bodies, their sexuality, and their relationship were explored, along with their intrapsychic reactions to the behavioral techniques.

The asymmetrical structure was utilized for the entire course of Emily and Dan's therapy, which lasted four months. During this time, there was a substantial improvement in their sexual relationship and a substantial decrease in each spouse's feelings of anxiety and frustration.

*Individually oriented.* Frank and Gail came for therapy because of a severe lack of intimacy in their marriage. Gail complained that Frank did not talk with her about his feelings and seemed disinterested in her feelings. Frank acknowledged that he had difficulty talking about his feelings, but also said that when he tried to do so, he experienced Gail as judgmental and critical of his efforts.

In their individual interviews, Frank and Gail explored the intrapsychic roots of their interpersonal problems. Frank was afraid that if he talked with Gail about his feelings he would appear weak, vulnerable, and unmanly. Gail was afraid that if she didn't frequently voice her frustration about Frank's lack of expressiveness, he would ignore her completely, thereby confirming her fear that she was unlovable. Each spouse's anxieties were closely linked to experiences in their families of origin.

Frank and Gail expressed a preference for meeting primarily in individual, rather than conjoint, interviews. They each felt that their relationship problems were mostly a result of internal conflicts and that each partner needed to work primarily at that level. Since the therapist agreed with their assessment, the therapy was structured as an individually oriented asymmetrical integration. Each spouse was seen for an individual interview once a week, with a conjoint interview scheduled once a month.

Frank's individual interviews were focused on helping him experience and express his emotions, particularly his sadness, anxiety, and anger. Gail's individual interviews were focused on helping her experience and understand the feelings of deprivation that lay beneath her chronic frustration and anger. Both spouses worked on transference issues in their relationship with each other and with the therapist.

In the conjoint interviews, work on improving their communication and problem-solving skills was the major focus. For this particular couple, a little of that went a long way. They were able to quickly improve the clarity of their communication and their ability to negotiate mutually acceptable behavior-change agreements. Implementing those agreements, however, required considerable individually oriented work.

The individually oriented structure was maintained over the course of one year. At that point, since there had been substantial improvement in their relationship, a plan for working toward termination was made. This plan involved decreasing the frequency of therapy meetings to once every two weeks, combining individual and conjoint interviews during each visit. This structure continued throughout the remaining six months of the therapy.

## Families—Symmetrical Integration

Alice, the 10-year-old girl with intense separation anxiety who was described in Chapter 1, and her parents were treated within the context of a symmetrical therapeutic structure. This type of structure was recommended because intrapsychic and interpersonal factors appeared to be equally important in the stimulation and reinforcement of Alice's anxiety. In order for this anxiety to be reduced, Alice needed to resolve the preconscious conflict between her need for her mother and her anger with her mother for withdrawing from her following the death of her own mother; and her need for her father and her fear of his angry outbursts. At the same time, Alice's mother needed to reduce her anxiety-stimulating intrusive behavior toward Alice; her father needed to reduce his anxiety-stimulating hostile behavior toward his wife and daughter; and both parents needed to reduce their anxiety-reinforcing over-protective reactions to Alice's symptoms.

Since neither Alice nor her parents expressed any negative reactions to either the individual or conjoint assessment interviews, a symmetrical therapeutic structure was recommended. One week, Alice was seen individually. The next week there was either a conjoint meeting with Alice and her parents or a meeting with the parents alone.

In the individual meetings with Alice, the focus was on helping her experience and work through her separation anxiety. The meetings with the parents were devoted to clarification of their feelings and thoughts about Alice's symptoms and about how each of them responded to her symptoms. The conjoint family meetings were focused on communication by each family member of positive and negative feelings about how things were going in the family and on efforts to negotiate constructive behavior-change agreements.

After about six months, there had been a substantial

improvement in Alice's symptoms. Therefore, the frequency of therapy meetings was reduced to once every two weeks. At that time, the alternating structure was changed to a combined one, which consisted of a 30-minute conjoint family meeting followed by a 30-minute individual meeting with Alice. This structure was maintained for the duration of the 12-month therapy.

### Families—Asymmetrical Integration

*Conjoint-oriented.* Seventeen-year-old Bill and his parents came for an evaluation because of the parents' concern about Bill's hostility toward them. The parents described Bill as oppositional and frequently belligerent, especially toward his mother. Bill's view of the situation was that his mother blamed his for all the problems between them and refused to look at her own considerable role in their conflicts. Father felt caught in the middle. His wife felt that he didn't support her in her efforts to discipline their son; Bill felt that his father was being manipulated by his mother to join her in unfairly blaming Bill.

The major problems presented by Bill and his parents were clearly interpersonal. Intrapsychic factors were certainly contributing to these interpersonal problems, but neither Bill nor his parents showed any genuine openness to exploring these intrapsychic issues. Therefore, a predominantly conjoint structure was recommended. Bill and his parents were seen conjointly for three weekly interviews in a row. On the fourth week, Bill was seen individually and his parents were seen conjointly. This structure was maintained for the duration of their therapy, which lasted six months.

In the conjoint family interviews, the focus was on problem identification, improving communication and problem-solving skills, and altering the family structure so that mother and son were less conflictually enmeshed, father and son were less disengaged, and the parenting alliance between mother and father was strengthened. In the individual interviews with Bill, the focus was on his cognitive distortions (e.g., seeing mother as the sole cause of all of his problems) and narcissistic vulnerability (feelings of inadequacy; fear of rejection by peers). In the interviews with the parents, attention was primarily directed toward clarification of their differing perspectives on how best to deal with Bill, their feelings about how each of them was interacting with him, and their feelings about how they were interacting with each other in relation to Bill.

At the time of termination, there was less hostility and more constructive dialogue between Bill and his mother, more open and direct communication between Bill and his father, and more constructive collaboration between the parents in their interactions with Bill.

*Individually oriented.* Mary, an 18-year-old high school senior, and her parents came for an evaluation because of the parents' concern about Mary's behavioral and emotional withdrawal, her lack of interest in previously enjoyable activities, and her "irresponsible" behavior (procrastination, forgetfulness, losing things).

In her initial individual interview, Mary was subdued, moderately depressed, and anxious. She talked of feelings of inadequacy in both the academic and social spheres, and she expressed serious doubts about her ability to succeed in college. She also talked about her parents' "nagging" and lack of flexibility in regard to her freedom of movement (e.g., curfew, staying at friends' houses overnight).

In the initial conjoint family interview, both parents were highly critical of Mary's "lack of responsibility" and concerned about her "spaced-out" moods. Mary again expressed a wish for less nagging and more flexibility from her parents.

Because Mary's problems appeared to be derived more from intrapsychic than interpersonal factors, an asymmetrical individually oriented structure was recommended. Mary came for individual interviews once a week, there was a conjoint family interview once a month; and brief (15 minute) telephone calls with the parents twice a month. This structure was maintained for four months, at which point Mary left for college. In the fall, there were two more individual meetings with Mary, preceded by brief telephone calls with her parents.

In the individual interviews, Mary's feelings of inadequacy, fear, and anger were explored and related to her conscious and preconscious cognitions (e.g., "I'm stupid"; "I'm ugly"; "No one is interested in being my friend"). These meetings were also used to help clarify her feelings in relation to her parents' behavior toward her and to work through her anxieties about communicating these feelings to them.

In the conjoint family meetings, Mary and her parents discussed positive and negative aspects of their relationship. Problems were reframed into specific requests for behavioral change and behavior-change agreements were negotiated. Mary agreed to take more responsibility around the house; her parents agreed to give her more freedom and to stop nagging her.

The telephone calls with the parents were used for communication by the parents of positive and negative feelings about Mary's behavior and communication by the therapist of positive and negative feelings about the parents' behavior with Mary.

The individually oriented structure was retained throughout the course of the therapy. At the time of termination, Mary was feeling more secure and confident about her ability to handle college. Her parents described her as less anxious, less depressed, and more self-assured.

### Promoting Therapeutic Change

By tailoring the treatment plan to fit the specific therapeutic needs and resistances of specific individuals and families, the therapist maximizes the possibilities for promoting individual and family interactional changes. As therapy progresses, the therapist monitors the extent to which the initial plan is facilitating the attainment of the family members' identified objectives. Based on the results of this monitoring, the original plan may be retained or it may be modified one or more times in response to changing individual or family interactional dynamics.

# 4

*Integrative Multilevel Model
of Therapeutic Change*

THERAPEUTIC CHANGE has been conceptualized by individual psychotherapists primarily in terms of processes for promoting intrapsychic changes (e.g., Carek, 1979; Luborsky, 1984; Meichenbaum, 1985) and by family therapists primarily in terms of processes for promoting behavioral changes (e.g., Aponte & VanDeusen, 1981; Gordon & Davidson, 1981; N.S. Jacobson, 1981). From an integrative multilevel perspective, both intrapsychic and behavioral change processes are highly significant. They are also complementary and synergistic. In this chapter, these two types of therapeutic change processes will be described and a model for their integration will be presented and illustrated with clinical examples.

## INTRAPSYCHIC CHANGE PROCESSES

### Insight and Working Through

Insight is the process whereby individuals acquire conscious awareness of previously unconscious feelings, thoughts, or behaviors (Moore & Fine, 1968). This process has generally been viewed as the major pathway to change in psychodynamic psychotherapy. Emotional insight, in which the new awareness contains both an affective and a cognitive component, is contrasted with intellectual insight, in which the affective component is missing. Significant therapeutic change is seen as primarily a function of emotional insight.

The new awareness produced by affective insight may relate to intrapsychic events (feelings and thoughts) or to interpersonal events (behaviors). The latter type of insight may pertain to the nature of one's behavior per se or it may focus on the effects of one's behavior on other people. For example, in working with conflictual couples and families, it is essential that the conflicting parties heighten their awareness of which aspects of their own behavior are stimulating negative reactions in other family members. They also need to heighten awareness of the nature of those negative reactions—that is, what feelings and thoughts their behavior is arousing in other family members.

Contrary to a common misunderstanding of the concept of insight (e.g., Stanton, 1981), the major focus of this process is always the immediate present, even when a particular insight relates to events from the past—for example, experiences in the family of origin. Insight about the past is helpful if, and only if, it promotes heightened awareness of current cognitive, emotional, or behavioral reality (Gill, 1982; Shapiro, 1989).

Working through is the process whereby repeated experiences of insight lead to lasting intrapsychic changes. As with insight itself, effective working through contains both an emotional and a cognitive component. The emotional component consists of two overlapping processes: (1) Repeated exposure, in a safe environment, to anxiety-producing internal stimuli (feelings, thoughts, images, memories, etc.). This exposure leads to anxiety reduction via desensitization (P. L. Wachtel, 1977); and (2) Repeated experiences of emotional catharsis, in which dysphoric emotions (e.g., sadness, guilt, shame, rage) are experienced and expressed in the context of an accepting and validating therapeutic relationship. Conscious awareness and non-traumatic expression of these emotional states help to reduce their intensity and promote exploration of the cognitive factors that stimulate their arousal.

The cognitive component of working through consists of gradually increasing understanding of the preconscious cognitive distortions, maladaptive schemata, and irrational conflicts that underlie emotional and behavioral dysfunction. This increased understanding prepares the way for the development of more adaptive cognitive processes.

## Cognitive Restructuring

Cognitive therapists (e.g., Beck, 1976; Ellis, 1973; Meichenbaum, 1985) have focused on the process of cognitive restructuring as the major mechanism of therapeutic change. This process is similar in some respects to insight and working through but differs from these processes in that it is more active and directive.

Initially, individuals learn to monitor their conscious and preconscious "automatic thoughts" (Beck, 1976) regarding self and others. Some of this monitoring takes place during therapy sessions, but the most important monitoring takes place during the course of day-to-day living.

### Clinical Illustration

A 16-year-old girl with bulimia learned to monitor her thoughts during those times when she felt a strong urge to binge. She became aware that when she was feeling anxious or depressed, she told herself that she "deserved" a binge because she was feeling so bad. She also told herself at those times that it was alright to binge because she could always "get rid of it" by purging. As she became aware of these cognitive processes, she realized that her bulimic behavior was, in part, a response to her thinking and that changing her thinking could help her change her behavior.

In addition to identifying dysfunctional cognitions, the process of cognitive restructuring also requires active countering and changing of such cognitions. Individuals learn to engage in change-promoting "internal dialogues" in which the more constructive components of the self actively question and combat the dysfunctional "self-statements" generated by the less constructive components. This process leads, over time, to a reduction in the frequency and intensity of dysfunctional cognitions and to the replacement of those cognitions by more functional ones.

### Clinical Illustration

The bulimic girl described in the preceding paragraph learned to counter her bulimia-stimulating automatic thoughts by telling herself that she "deserved" not to be bulimic and that purging behavior was not alright because it was dangerous to her health. At first, these thoughts were met with internal resistance (e.g., "one binge isn't going to hurt me"), but gradually she was able to overcome the resistances, using the new cognitions to help decrease her bulimic behavior.

Some cognitive therapists (e.g., Meichenbaum, 1985) have emphasized the importance of "self-instructions training," in which individuals learn to "coach" themselves by developing positive internal self-instructions and self-reinforcements. Learning to coach oneself in more constructive responding leads to an increased ability to inhibit dysfunctional responses (e.g., impulsive or hostile behavior) and to substitute more constructive ones (e.g., thoughtful, assertive behavior) (Kendall & Braswell, 1985; Novaco, 1975). Examples of positive self-instructions are "Take it easy"; "Don't take this personally"; "What am I supposed to do now?"; "What's the best way to solve this problem?"; "I did a good job."

## Internalization

The most global type of intrapsychically oriented change process is internalization. In a change-promoting therapeutic relationship, the therapist relates to the patient with empathy, respect, concern, and genuineness (Rogers, 1980); helps the patient experience and understand the emotional and cognitive factors underlying his or her dysfunctional behavior; and stimulates and reinforces constructive cognitive, emotional, and behavioral changes. As therapy proceeds, the therapist's empathic, supporting, confronting, and reinforcing behaviors are internalized and the patient begins to relate to him- or herself as he or she has experienced the therapist relating to him or her. Over time, this leads to enduring changes in the patient's attitudes and feelings about him- or herself and his or her relationships with other people.

## BEHAVIORAL CHANGE PROCESSES

### Desensitization

Behavioral desensitization (Rimm & Cunningham, 1985; Wolpe, 1958) is the process whereby individuals learn to reduce maladaptive avoidance behavior by exposing themselves to feared external situations or objects (e.g., shopping malls, heights, public speaking, tests, animals) in such a way that their anxiety, and thus their avoidance behavior, is reduced. In *imaginal desensitization*, the exposure takes place via imagined images of the feared situation or object. In *in vivo desensitization*, there is direct exposure to the actual feared situation or object. Relaxation techniques are used to help individuals maintain the exposure long enough for desensitization to occur. Family members often accompany the symptomatic individual during in vivo desensitization to offer support and encouragement.

## Suggestion

Behavioral suggestions stimulate behavioral change by encouraging individuals or families to try new behaviors. Such suggestions may be direct or indirect.

Direct suggestions are straightforward. The therapist suggests a decrease in dysfunctional behavior and/or an increase in functional behavior. For instance, he or she may suggest to a man with an anger control problem that he ask for a time-out whenever he feels himself starting to get angry; a child with nocturnal enuresis may receive a suggestion not to drink anything between dinner and bedtime; each partner in a conflictual couple may be asked to keep track of those things that the other person does that he or she experiences as pleasing. When accompanied by a clear rationale and ample opportunity for discussion and feedback, such suggestions are highly effective ways to stimulate behavioral changes. When there is resistance to following a direct behavioral suggestion, the sources of this resistance are explored. This information is then used to guide future behavioral suggestions.

Indirect suggestions are paradoxical; they prescribe continuing or increasing dysfunctional behaviors and/or avoiding functional behaviors. For example, the therapist might suggest to a person with insomnia that he or she deliberately try to stay awake as long as possible; a family with a high level of parent-child conflict might be asked to schedule arguments for specific times during the week. When individuals or families follow such suggestions, they are often able to gain a sense of mastery and control over behaviors previously experienced as uncontrollable. This sense of control helps to reduce feelings of helplessness and paves the way for subsequent positive behavioral changes.

When there is resistance to a paradoxical suggestion, constructive behavioral change may result. For example, the insomniac may resist trying to stay awake by falling asleep; the conflictual family may resist the suggestion to schedule conflicts by becoming less conflictual. These changes are clearly desirable; however, it is extremely important that the therapist refrain from making paradoxical suggestions that he or she does not genuinely believe will be beneficial if carried out. For example, suicidal people should not be encouraged to increase suicidal behavior, nor should people with anger control problems be encouraged to increase aggressive behavior.

### Modeling and Rehearsal

In addition to suggestion, behavioral changes can be stimulated by the processes of modeling and behavior rehearsal. Each of these processes can be utilized in both individual and family interviews.

Modeling is the social learning process whereby one person (the observer) alters his or her behavior so that it more closely approximates that of another person (the model). In working with individuals, role-play modeling by the therapist is used to help in the acquisition of new behavioral skills, such as, assertiveness, empathy, emotional expressiveness, approaching feared situations, and so forth.

With families, therapist modeling stimulates the acquisition of such skills both directly and indirectly. Whoever the therapist interacts with during a role play is directly affected by the therapist's behavior. Whoever may be observing the role play is indirectly affected by seeing his or her ways of interacting with the other family member(s). Both types of effects stimulate changes in family interactional patterns.

Modeling is generally used in conjunction with behavior rehearsal. With individuals, behavior rehearsal occurs in the context of a role-play interaction with the therapist. By rehearsing new behaviors within the safe environment of the therapeutic relationship, the individual develops the confidence to begin behaving in new ways with people other than the therapist—for example, members of his or her family.

With families, behavior rehearsal takes place directly among the family members. Initially, this rehearsal occurs during therapy sessions, where the therapist monitors the process, giving instructions and feedback. Later, family members practice newly acquired behaviors outside of therapy, with indirect monitoring and feedback from the therapist.

## Reinforcement

The therapist's responses to observed or reported behaviors are reinforcing when they maintain or increase the probability of those behaviors recurring. Generally, two types of behavioral changes are reinforced: (1) positive process behavior—for example, monitoring and recording functional and dysfunctional behaviors; participating in a role-play exercise; and (2) positive outcome behavior—for example, making progress toward individual or familial therapeutic goals.

With individuals, reinforcement by the therapist leads over time to self-reinforcement. With families, reinforcement by the therapist is supplemented (and eventually replaced) by the reinforcements that family members learn to give to each other.

## INTEGRATION

Intrapsychic and behavioral changes and change processes are complementary and synergistic (Feldman, 1976b; 1989; Kramer, 1980; P.L. Wachtel, 1977; Wachtel & Wachtel, 1986). Each type of change and each type of change process facilitates and strengthens the other. When there is a block to change at one level, it can frequently be reduced or eliminated by change at the other level. In the following sections, the interactions between intrapsychic and behavioral change processes will be discussed and illustrated with clinical examples.

### Using Intrapsychic Change Processes to Facilitate Behavioral Changes

Behavioral changes in family systems are frequently blocked by the dysfunctional cognitions and emotions of individual family members. When these intrapsychic factors are neglected, therapy often becomes bogged down in frustratingly repetitious efforts to promote change by means of behavioral change processes alone. Reduction or elimination of the intrapsychic blocks allows behavioral change to proceed.

## *Clinical Illustrations*

(1) Barbara and Bill, the conflictual couple described in Chapter 1, were unable to learn effective problem-solving skills because each spouse blamed the other for their marital problems, did not listen to the other person's complaints, and refused to initiate any behavioral changes. Barbara correctly identified Bill's passive-aggressive behavior (e.g., coming home late and not calling; forgetting to pay bills) as a problem, but she had great difficulty acknowledging that her own behavior (harsh criticism; threats of divorce) was also a problem. Conversely, Bill correctly identified the contribution that his wife's behavior was making to their marital problems but he minimized the importance of his own behavior.

Underlying these perceptual distortions were preconscious anxieties. Each spouse was afraid that if he or she acknowledged his or her role in creating and maintaining the marital problems, the other spouse would not reciprocate and he or she would be labeled as "the cause" of their problems. These anxieties stemmed, in part, from the other spouse's attitude and behavior and, in part, from each person's own feelings of narcissistic vulnerability, based on experiences in their families of origin.

In individual interviews with Barbara and Bill, intrapsychic change processes (insight, working through, and cognitive restructuring) were utilized to decrease each spouse's resistance to accepting responsibility for his or her role in maintaining the marital problems. Over time, both spouses were able to reduce their defensiveness. As they did so, they were increasingly able to make use of conjoint interviews and behavioral change processes (suggestion, modeling, rehearsal) to develop constructive problem-solving interactions.

(2) The father of a 12-year-old boy with behavior control problems was resistant to the therapist's suggestions about setting firmer limits and imposing more substantial consequences for rule-breaking behavior. As he discussed his feelings about his relationship with his son, the father came to the realization that he was afraid to discipline him because he feared that if he did so his son would no longer love him. This anxiety stemmed, in large part, from his childhood experience with his own father, who had been excessively demanding and punitive with him. As he worked through his feelings about his relationship with his father, he was increasingly able to make use of the therapist's suggestions about his own parenting. Gradually, he was able to develop more consistent and effective parenting behaviors.

(3) A couple sought marital therapy because of a lack of intimacy in their relationship. Positive interactions were few and far between. Physical affection was minimal; sex was nonexistent. The wife's main complaint was that her husband didn't talk with her about his feelings. The husband's main complaint was that his wife was unaffectionate and sexually unresponsive.

In individual interviews, each spouse's anxieties, conflicts, and defenses were explored. It soon became clear that the husband's avoidance of emotional communication and the wife's avoidance of physical affection and sexuality were both based on preconscious feelings of anxiety. The husband was afraid that if he revealed his feelings to his wife, particularly feelings of fear or sadness, she would experience him as a "weak" person and would abandon him. The wife was afraid that if she allowed herself to be affectionate and sexual, she would be "swallowed up" by her husband and would lose her sense of separateness and autonomy.

Each spouse's defenses against his or her own anxiety triggered anxiety in the other. The husband's inhibition in the area of emotional communication stimulated in his wife an unconscious image of him as a cold, powerful, and dangerous person. This image reinforced her fear of being taken over if she were to let down her guard sexually. The wife's inhibition in the area of affection and sexuality stimulated the husband's fear that he was an unattractive, weak person. The arousal of this fear strengthened his expressive inhibition.

Individual interviews with each spouse were utilized to explore the anxieties and cognitive distortions that stimulated their dysfunctional marital behaviors. The husband became aware of his preconscious fear of being abandoned by his wife and of the connections between this fear and his more deeply unconscious fear of being abandoned by his mother. The wife became aware of her preconscious fear of being dominated by her husband and of the connections between this fear and her more deeply unconscious fear of being dominated by her father. As these emotional issues were explored, each spouse's anxiety began to decrease.

As their anxieties diminished, they were able to utilize conjoint interviews to develop more effective communication and problem-solving behaviors and to negotiate and implement constructive behavior-change agreements. The husband increased his emotional communication; the wife increased her affectionate and sexual behavior. They both reported a substantial increase in marital satisfaction.

(4) A 16-year-old girl and her parents came for therapy because of frequent dysfunctional conflicts between the girl and her mother. These conflicts generally took the form of the mother becoming enraged with her daughter when she "broke the rules"—for example, talking too long on the telephone, staying out past curfew. During these conflicts, mother and daughter were each verbally abusive toward the other. The father's role during those times was primarily that of mediator between his wife and daughter.

In individual interviews, the daughter was helped to experience and to understand the feelings and thoughts that were stimulating her oppositional behavior. She said that she felt smothered by her mother and desperately wanted to be more independent of her. It was pointed out to her that her oppositional behavior was having the opposite effect—the more oppositional she was, the more involved her mother was in her affairs. As this pattern was explored, she began to realize that in addition to her conscious desire to separate from her mother there was also a good deal of preconscious separation anxiety. By stimulating her mother's overinvolvement she had been masking her anxiety about separating from her. Over time, she was able to reduce this anxiety and develop more constructive ways of separating from her mother.

In interviews with the parents, they each became aware of feeling frustrated and angry with the other. Mother felt undermined by her husband because he didn't unequivocally support her efforts to discipline their daughter. Father felt that his wife overreacted to the daughter's oppositional behavior and that she unfairly put him in the middle of their arguments. As these feelings were explored, the parents were able to respond to communication and problem-solving techniques to develop a more constructive and collaborative approach to parenting their daughter.

## Using Behavioral Change Processes to Facilitate Intrapsychic Changes

Intrapsychic changes by individual family members are often blocked by dysfunctional behavioral processes in the family. When these interpersonal blocks are ignored, therapeutic insights are not translated into lasting intrapsychic changes. Reduction or elimination of the interpersonal blocks allows intrapsychic change processes to proceed.

### Clinical Illustrations

(1) A 30-year-old woman had been hospitalized on multiple occasions for suicidal depression. Medication and individual psychotherapy led to temporary improvement but

not long-term change. After repeated relapses, she and her husband were referred for marital therapy.

In conjoint interviews, it soon became apparent that this patient's depressive symptoms were being stimulated and reinforced, in part, by a dysfunctional interactional pattern between her and her husband. When she was feeling less depressed and began functioning more effectively, he complained that she was neglecting him. This led to a series of intense, dysfunctional arguments and stimulated guilt feelings in the wife. Soon, she began to feel more depressed and to function less effectively. When that happened, her husband became very concerned and solicitous, thus reinforcing the depressive symptoms.

In marital therapy, the spouses learned to deal with their conflicts in more constructive ways and to alter their habitual ways of responding to the other's behavior. The husband began to reinforce his wife's effective, nondepressed behavior and to be less "hovering" when she expressed feelings of depression. The wife became more sensitive to her husband's vulnerabilities and began to pay more attention to him when she was feeling better. Each spouse's behavioral changes reinforced those of the other.

As the interactional pattern changed, the wife was able to utilize insight and working through to resolve the intrapsychic conflicts related to the experiences in her family of origin that had been contributing to her repeated depressions. At the same time, her husband was able to utilize these same change processes to resolve his own intrapsychic conflicts, which had been masked by his wife's depressions.

(2) An 11-year-old boy and his family were referred for therapy because of the boy's failing grades in school and

his hostile attitude at home. His parents were divorced and he lived primarily with his mother. During the previous year he had been in individual therapy, which had led to little behavioral or emotional change.

During the assessment process, it became clear that this boy was extremely angry with his father for having "abandoned" him after the divorce. Therefore, arrangements were made for him and his father to meet conjointly. Initially, the father was defensive but soon began to respond to his son's feelings of abandonment by increasing the amount of time that he spent with him and by increasing the amount of attention that he paid to his son's day-to-day activities. As he did so, the boy began to realize that he had been acting out his angry feelings toward his father by means of passive-aggressive behavior at school and hostile behavior at home. He also began to realize that this was self-defeating and to translate this realization into behavioral change.

(3) A couple came for therapy because of frequent dysfunctional conflicts. In the initial conjoint interview, they indicated that they were arguing almost daily and were unable to resolve any of the issues they argued about. Their communication in the interview consisted almost entirely of mutual accusations and blaming.

In individual interviews, it became clear that each spouse was experiencing a great deal of narcissistic vulnerability. Each was so fearful of being injured by the other that he or she was unable to mobilize even a minimal amount of empathy for the other's feelings or needs. Efforts to help them explore their feelings of vulnerability were repeatedly blocked by negative statements about the other.

In subsequent conjoint interviews, the spouses were asked to talk with each other about their feelings and to really listen to each other. When one tried to interrupt, he or she was reminded about the necessity for active, empathic listening. Empathic listening and empathic responding were modeled during role-play interactions with each of them.

Over time, they began to listen to each other and gradually developed a capacity for empathy. As they did so, they were able to use individual interviews to focus on their own narcissistic vulnerabilities and to explore the roots of this vulnerability in their families of origin. This process led to a reduction in each spouse's feelings of vulnerability, and to an increase in their capacity to interact with each other in affirming and enjoyable ways.

(4) A 10-year-old girl and her family came for therapy because of the girl's school failure and emotional withdrawal. In an individual interview, the girl indicated that she had been feeling lonely and increasingly depressed for about six months. During that period of time her father had lost his job and her mother had begun working full time outside of the home. As a result, both parents became less available than they had been—mother because of her increased work hours and father because of his depression about his job loss. The daughter was feeling abandoned by both of her parents.

In an interview with the parents, several behavioral changes were suggested. The first suggestion was that father take on more responsibility for tasks involving his daughter, such as, arranging after-school activities, driving her to and from friends' houses, and so forth. The second suggestion was that mother call home each day to talk with her daughter when she came home from school. The third suggestion was that the parents arrange their weekend schedules so that they could spend as much time as possible with their daughter, separately and together.

As the parents began to implement these behavioral changes, there were a number of intrapsychic shifts. Father's increased responsibility in relation to his daughter helped to reduce the feelings of inadequacy that had been generated by his job loss. Mother's increased contact with her daughter helped to reduce her guilt about returning to work full time. Daughter began to feel less depressed, more able to concentrate on her work at school, and more comfortable and secure with both of her parents.

## Interrupting Multilevel Problem-Maintenance Loops

As discussed in Chapter 1, individual and family interactional problems are maintained by multilevel feedback loops. In order to interrupt these feedback loops, both intrapsychic and behavioral changes are needed.

In some instances, change at one level will lead directly to change at the other. For example, anxiety reduction in one or more family members may reduce defensive behavior and thus lead to family interactional changes. Conversely, family interactional changes may lead to reduced anxiety and defensiveness in one or more family members.

Often, however, change at one level is blocked by lack of change at the other. For example, anxiety reduction in one family member may prove to be temporary because of a lack of behavioral change by other family members. Conversely, family interactional change may prove to be temporary because of the unchanged anxieties of one or more family members. By utilizing an integrated combination of intrapsychic and behavioral change processes, blocks at each level can be reduced or eliminated.

# 5

*Integrating Individual and Family Therapy Techniques*

In order to most effectively promote both intrapsychic and interpersonal change processes, an integration of individual and family therapy techniques is needed. Both types of intervention have specific strengths and specific limitations. Individually oriented techniques are the most effective means for promoting intrapsychic changes; family-oriented techniques are the most effective means for promoting family interactional changes. Integration of these techniques allows the therapist to utilize the strengths of each and to tailor the therapy to meet the specific needs of particular individuals and families.

In the following sections, individual therapy techniques derived from the psychodynamic (Baker, 1985), cognitive (Meichenbaum, 1985), and behavioral (Rimm & Cunningham, 1985) approaches and family therapy techniques derived from the structural (Minuchin & Fishman, 1981), behavioral (Gordon & Davidson, 1981; N. S. Jacobson, 1981), and strategic (Stanton, 1981) approaches will be described. These techniques were selected on the basis of their clinical and research validation. After describing the techniques, methods for their integration will be presented and illustrated with clinical examples.

## INDIVIDUAL THERAPY TECHNIQUES

### Clarification

Clarification is designed to enhance the therapist's and patient's understanding of the patient's conscious and pre-conscious emotions and cognitions. The process of clarification involves the use of *empathic listening, empathic questioning*, and *empathic reflecting*.

Empathic questions and reflections may pertain to immediate, in-therapy feelings and thoughts or they may pertain to previously experienced, extratherapy feelings and thoughts. In both instances, the objectives of clarification are to illuminate the nature of the patient's subjective experience and to establish a therapeutic alliance based on accurate empathy, concern, and nonjudgmental respect.

### Confrontation

Confrontation is the process whereby the therapist points out those aspects of an individual's cognitive, emotional, or behavioral reactions that appear to be incomplete, exaggerated, or unrealistic. Whenever possible, it is helpful to precede a confrontation with a statement validating those aspects of the individual's feelings, thoughts, and behaviors that appear to be realistic and reasonable responses to internal or external events. For example: (1) "I agree with you that your son often behaves irresponsibly; however, I do not agree that he never behaves responsibly"; (2) "Yes, your wife's behavior is a major cause of the problems in your marriage. However, your behavior is an equally important cause of those problems"; (3) "I understand why you're angry with your parents and I agree they are sometimes too strict with you. However, I think your anger at times is excessive and stops you from being able to problem solve with them"; (4) "I think you are a good deal more angry than you are aware of".

Confrontations promote therapeutic change by challenging defensive distortions of external and internal reality. They also set the stage for dynamic and genetic interpretations.

## Interpretation

Therapeutic interpretations are inferential hypotheses about the connections between an individual's behavior, conscious emotions, or conscious cognitions and his or her preconscious or unconscious emotions and cognitions. Interpretations may be focused entirely on current reality (dynamic interpretations), or they may suggest connections between present and past reality (genetic interpretations). Examples of dynamic interpretations are: "I suspect that underneath your anger is a lot of hurt"; "I believe you feel depressed because the self-critical part of you keeps telling you how worthless you are." Examples of genetic interpretations are "When your husband is distant, I think it touches off in you some very painful feelings about how distant your mother was when you were growing up"; "Whenever your mom gets sick, I think it reminds you of when she had to go to the hospital when you were a little boy and how scary that was for you."

Transference interpretations focus on the patient's conscious and preconscious feelings and thoughts about the current important relationships in his or her life and the connections between these relationships and the important relationships in his or her family of origin. One form of transference interpretation focuses on current family relationships; another form focuses on the relationship with the therapist. Examples of the first type of transference interpretation are given in the preceding paragraph. Examples of the second type are: "It sounds like you feel hurt and angry about my upcoming vacation"; "I think that part of why you're feeling so hurt and angry about my leaving is because you were left so often by your parents when you were little."

The data upon which interpretations are based include overt behavior (verbal and nonverbal), conscious feelings and thoughts, and dreams. In working with dreams, a number of different techniques are available. In the classical psychoanalytic method (Grinstein, 1983), the dreamer describes the dream and then reports whatever feelings and thoughts enter his or her conscious awareness as he or she focuses on the dream as a whole or on specific elements of the dream. In the gestalt therapy method (Perls, 1970), the dreamer is asked to describe the dream in the present tense, as if it were happening here and now, and then to take the role of the various elements of the dream and describe his or her feelings and thoughts as that dream element. The gestalt method can be a powerful means for heightening emotional experiencing, but it often stimulates a higher degree of anxiety than the psychoanalytic method. For this reason, it is usually most helpful to begin with the free-association technique and to add the role-playing technique later.

With children, interpretations are often based on play behavior. Initially, such interpretations are made in relation to the play—for example, "I bet the little bear is mad at his father for leaving him that way"; "The girl in that picture looks like she's feeling very sad". Later, a shift may be made to the child—for example, "I wonder if you sometimes feel mad at your father"; "I think you felt sad like that when your mother had to go to the hospital."

## Cognitive Monitoring

Cognitive monitoring is a process designed to heighten conscious awareness of dysfunctional cognitions. The process begins with an explanation by the therapist about the relationship between behavioral and emotional symptoms and conscious and preconscious cognitive processes. The therapist then asks the individual to focus on the cognitive processes that are associated with his or her emotional experiences during the therapy sessions and to monitor and record the cognitions that are associated with his or her emotional and/or behavioral symptoms in between therapy sessions. In the early stages of therapy, the focus of cognitive monitoring is on conscious and preconscious automatic thoughts. Later, the focus shifts to more deeply unconscious irrational beliefs and assumptions, which are revealed by the common themes that emerge over time from the monitoring of automatic thoughts.

## Cognitive Restructuring

In addition to monitoring their cognitions, individuals are also asked to examine these cognitions in terms of their accuracy, specificity, and rationality. The therapist seeks to establish a collaborative process, working together with the individual to identify those ways in which his or her cognitions are functional or dysfunctional. In doing this, it is important that the therapist focus on the rational, as well as the irrational, components of the cognitive processes that are being examined and that he or she acknowledge and validate these elements. When this part of the process is ignored, the therapy is often experienced as an attack, rather than a supportive collaboration.

The cognitive examination process is applied to cognitions that occur during therapy sessions and to those that occur between therapy sessions. In each instance, individuals are asked to use their emotional and behavioral symptoms as signals to search for preconscious symptom-stimulating cognitions and to subject these cognitions to intensive rational analysis. An example of this process occurred in the therapy of the bulimic girl described in Chapter 4, when she became aware that her symptoms were being stimulated, in part, by the automatic thoughts, "I deserve a binge because I feel so bad" and "It's alright to binge because I can get rid of it by throwing up." As she subjected these thoughts to cognitive examination, she began to realize how irrational and self-defeating they were.

The final step in the cognitive restructuring process is the generation of constructive alternatives to the identified and examined dysfunctional cognitions. Individuals are asked to write down constructive alternatives to their dysfunctional cognitions and to pay close attention to the feelings and thoughts that arise in response to these constructive alternatives. Negative reactions are then subjected to the same process of collaborative empiricism that was previously used to examine the original dysfunctional cognition. In this way, resistances to cognitive change are gradually reduced, paving the way for the establishment of more constructive cognitive processes. For example, the bulimic girl referred to above was able to generate the constructive alternative cognition, "I deserve to be healthy, and binging and throwing up are not healthy." Initially, there was considerable internal resistance to this cognition, but with practice this resistance was overcome.

### Self-instruction Training

The technique of self-instruction training is related to cognitive restructuring but the identification of dysfunctional cognitions is not involved (Meichenbaum, 1985). Rather, the therapist teaches individuals to coach themselves by learning to generate internal self-instructions under specific stressful circumstances (e.g., test-taking, marital arguments, etc.). The therapist does this by first modeling the process of giving self-instructions, then helping the individual practice doing this him- or herself. Initially, self-instructions are given out loud. Then, they are given in a whisper. Finally, they are given silently. Some examples of self-instructions are "I can handle this"; "Slow down"; "Take a deep breath"; "What are my choices?"; "What's the best choice?"

## Behavioral Desensitization

Systematic behavioral desensitization begins with the construction of a fear hierarchy, ranging from the least feared to the most feared elements of a phobic situation or object. Then, relaxation techniques—such as, progressive muscle relaxation (E. Jacobson, 1938)—are taught. When the individual is in a relaxed state, he or she is asked to imagine the least feared image from the fear hierarchy. If anxiety is experienced, the person is asked either to stop imagining the scene (Wolpe, 1958) or to relax the anxiety away (Goldfried, 1971). When a scene can be imagined for 20 to 25 seconds without conscious anxiety, the process moves on to the next higher scene on the fear hierarchy. When all scenes can be held in awareness without anxiety, the process is completed.

In vivo systematic desensitization involves the same principles as imaginal desensitization; but, instead of being imagined, the scenes are directly experienced. For example, a school-avoidant child would be helped to create a hierarchy of feared images associated with going to school—walking to school, waiting for school to start, working in the classroom, and so forth. The child would then be asked to actually experience each of these scenes, starting with the least anxiety-producing one and progressing to the most anxiety-producing one. One or more family members would be asked to accompany the child during these experiences to provide support, encouragement, and affirmation.

## Behavioral Suggestion

In making direct suggestions, the therapist recommends an increase in specific functional behaviors or a decrease in specific dysfunctional behaviors. For example, the therapist might suggest to a depressed woman that she start a regular program of physical exercise; a couple with sexual problems might receive the suggestion that they begin doing sensate focus exercises; the parents of a child with behavior control problems might receive specific suggestions for effectively using limit-setting and behavioral consequences. If there is resistance to following a direct behavioral suggestion, the therapist explores the sources of the resistance and uses the information obtained by this exploration to guide future behavioral suggestions.

When conscious or unconscious resistance to direct suggestion is very high, indirect (paradoxical) suggestions can be helpful. In making a paradoxical suggestion, the therapist explains that sometimes the best way to change something is to actively try not to change it or even to try to make it worse. The therapist then asks the individual to do actively that which he or she has been experiencing as "uncontrollable." When such prescriptions are followed, there is an increase in feelings of mastery and control and a decrease in feelings of helplessness. If the prescription is not followed, the therapist explores the reasons for the resistance and again explains the rationale for the prescription.

At times, resistance to a paradoxical suggestion leads to positive behavioral change. However, as noted in Chapter 4, the therapist should not assume that a paradoxical suggestion will necessarily be resisted. Therefore, such suggestions should only be given when the therapist is completely comfortable with the possibility that the suggestion will, in fact, be carried out.

### Modeling and Behavior Rehearsal

Therapist modeling is a useful technique for helping individuals develop or strengthen behavioral skills—such as, assertiveness, empathy, emotional expressiveness, and so forth. It is important that the therapist not only model the desired behavior, but that he or she also model specific strategies for coping with the problems that are interfering with the individual's ability to behave in the desired way. For example, if an individual is inhibited in the area of assertiveness because he or she is afraid of being attacked in response to an assertive act, the therapist models strategies for coping with this possibility, in addition to modeling the initial assertive behavior.

After modeling a new behavior, the therapist asks the

individual to "try it out" in the context of a role-played behavior rehearsal. The individual's efforts are responded to with positive feedback, behavioral suggestions, additional modeling, and/or additional behavior rehearsal.

## Behavioral Reinforcement

The therapist reinforces observed or reported positive behavioral changes. Such reinforcement may be verbal (e.g., "that's great") or nonverbal (e.g., a smile or head nod). Over time, external reinforcement from the therapist is internalized, leading to an increased capacity for self-reinforcement.

## FAMILY THERAPY TECHNIQUES

## Joining

The therapist joins a family system by communicating to the family via his or her verbal and nonverbal behavior that he or she understands them, values them, and is committed to and capable of helping them change. Initially, the therapist listens empathically and respectfully to each family member's view of the family's problems and strengths. Then, he or she validates some aspect of what each person has said. Since family members are often in conflict, validation of one person's view may be threatening to one or more of the others. Therefore, it is essential that the therapist distribute his or her validations equally among the family members (Feldman, 1976c).

Another important aspect of joining is "meeting the family where they're at." The therapist's initial goal is to identify the family's problems and strengths *as seen by the family members*. The only objective at this stage is understanding and relationship building. Later, once he or she has joined with the family, the therapist is in a position to effectively challenge dysfunctional perceptions or interactional patterns.

**Enactment**

Enactment is the process whereby the therapist asks two or more family members to interact directly with one another during a therapy meeting. This interaction may be limited to verbal discussion—for example, "Please discuss this directly with each other"—or there may be a more active behavioral component—for example, "Mrs. Jones, please stop Patty from hitting her sister." In some instances, enactments may be brief (e.g., a one-minute dialogue between a husband and wife); in other instances, they may be quite lengthy (e.g., an anorexic girl and her family may be asked to eat lunch together during the therapy hour).

With both brief and lengthy enactments, the therapist observes the family members' interactions and, on the basis of these observations, formulates hypotheses about the structural aspects of the family system that are contributing to individual and interpersonal problems. The therapist then formulates interventions to help change these dysfunctional structures.

### Family Restructuring

Restructuring interventions are designed to stimulate changes in family boundaries or family roles. When these are excessively firm, the therapist attempts to stimulate increased flexibility; when they are excessively flexible, he or she attempts to stimulate increased firmness.

One way of stimulating structural change is by commenting on dysfunctional boundaries or roles and suggesting that change is needed. For example, the therapist might say, "Mr. Johnson, I think part of the reason why your son is depressed is that he feels there is a wall between you and him. I think you could help reduce that feeling by initiating more contact with him, especially around things that you both like to do." In this intervention, the therapist comments on the rigid boundary between the father and son and suggests increased contact as a way of reducing boundary rigidity.

The therapist can also stimulate structural changes by defining rules of interaction (e.g., no interruptions, each person talks for him- or herself) and by directing family members to interact with one another in ways that are counter to the existing structure. For instance, with a family in which father and daughter are enmeshed and mother is disengaged, the therapist might ask mother and daughter to talk directly to each other while father and therapist observe.

## Problem-solving Training

Problem-solving training is designed to help couples and families develop more constructive methods for defining and solving their problems. Initially, family members are helped to specify problems in clear, behaviorally specific language, to translate problem statements into requests for behavioral change, and to clearly express the reasons for their requests. For example: (1) A wife asked her husband to stop yelling at her when he got angry. She explained that she was asking him to make this change because "when you yell at me, I feel like you hate me"; (2) A father asked his son to do his homework every day. He said that he was making this request because "I love you and I want you to be successful"; (3) A daughter asked her mother to stop asking her so many questions about her social life. She explained that "when you do that, I feel like you don't trust me."

In response to a request for change, the person of whom the request is being made is asked to communicate his or her feelings and thoughts about the request to the person or persons making the request. The therapist coaches the responder to: (1) actively think about the request and the reasons for the request; (2) actively empathize with the expressed feelings of the requester(s); (3) communicate his or her understanding of what is being requested; and (4) express his or her feelings and thoughts about the request in a constructive (noninsulting, nondiscounting) way.

The therapist counters dysfunctional blaming of other family members by emphasizing that each person's behavior is contributing to the family problems and that each person's behavior needs to change in order for those problems to be resolved. Then, the therapist helps each family member identify those changes that he or she is willing to make. When all family members have agreed to one or more specific behavioral changes, the therapist underlines the importance of each person taking responsibility for initiating behavioral change, rather than waiting for the other family member(s) to change first. The therapist also emphasizes the importance of family members noticing and positively reinforcing other family members' behavioral changes.

Subsequent to a behavior-change agreement, the therapist monitors the implementation process. When positive behavioral change is reported he or she reinforces that change, in verbal and/or nonverbal ways. When noncompliance is reported, the therapist explores with the couple or family the reasons for the noncompliance and helps them either work through the resistance to the original agreement or negotiate a new agreement.

## Parenting Skills Training

Behavioral parenting skills training focuses on helping parents increase constructive parenting behaviors and decrease nonconstructive ones. Initially, the therapist emphasizes the importance of positive reinforcement for desirable behavior and helps the parents increase the frequency and range of their reinforcing responses. Then, attention is focused on increasing the clarity and consistency of the parents' communication of behavioral expectations and rules. Following this, the parents are helped to pinpoint (identify in behaviorally specific language) their child's behavioral problems and to develop effective consequences in response to problem behaviors.

Parents are taught the principles of "time out," which involves either the temporary removal of reinforcing activities (e.g., "no television for the next hour") or the temporary removal of the child from reinforcing surroundings (e.g., "sit on the steps for the next 20 minutes"). They are also taught how to use contingent release from time out (e.g., "You may get off the stairs as soon as you stop yelling"; "You will be allowed to watch television again when you have finished your homework").

The methods of behavioral parenting training include (1) an explanation of the principles of reinforcement and punishment; (2) feedback about constructive and nonconstructive aspects of the parents' behavior; (3) instructions about and modeling of effective parenting behaviors; (4) behavior rehearsal; and (5) positive reinforcement of constructive changes. Much of the work of this type of training is carried out in meetings with the parents only. However, it is important that the therapist also directly observe behavioral interactions between the parents and the symptomatic child or adolescent and intervene directly when necessary.

The effectiveness of behavioral parenting training is often limited by the presence of marital problems and/or individual problems of one or both parents. The therapist needs to identify such problems when they exist and help the parents find effective ways to overcome them.

## Reframing

The strategic technique of reframing is designed to shift the conceptual framework within which family members view their situation. One way the therapist can accomplish this is by asking about family strengths. Often, family members are so focused on their problems that they forget about their strengths. When family members' attention is directed by the therapist to those aspects of family life they are feeling good about, their perspective shifts in a positive direction. If family members are not able to identify current strengths, the therapist focuses on past strengths. This shift introduces the hopeful possibility of recapturing positive aspects of family life that were present at one time but are currently being blocked by dysfunctional interactions.

A second type of reframing involves the use of positive connotation. Here, the therapist attempts to identify positive aspects of dysfunctional interactions. For example, a conflictual couple may be told that part of why their arguments become so intense is that they care so much about their relationship. Similarly, a boy who argues incessantly with his parents about the rules he must follow may be told that his willingness to stand up for his rights is admirable but that he needs to learn more effective ways of getting what he wants. By introducing this type of positive perspective, the therapist fosters a shift away from negativity and hopelessness and toward collaboration and constructive problem solving.

**Paradoxical Suggestions**

With families, paradoxical suggestions are used to help family members gain control over their interactions by actively attempting to continue doing what they have been doing but in a different way. For example, a highly conflictual family may be asked to schedule specific times for fighting during the week; a highly conflict-avoidant family may be asked to actively resist talking with each other about any negative feelings. As with individuals, when families follow such suggestions, they begin to gain a sense of mastery and control over their problem. When they resist, positive behavioral changes may result. For instance, the conflictual family may resist scheduling conflicts by becoming less conflictual; the conflict-avoidant family may resist actively avoiding talking about negative feelings by starting to talk about such feelings. However, as previously noted, the therapist should only make a paradoxical suggestion when he or she genuinely believes that the family will benefit by carrying out the suggestion.

## INTEGRATION

Individual and family therapy techniques are complementary and synergistic. Each type of technique has the potential to extend and enhance the effectiveness of the other. By utilizing an integrated combination of individual and family therapy techniques, the therapist greatly increases his or her ability to establish and maintain effective therapeutic alliances and to effectively promote both individual and family interactional changes.

### Establishing and Maintaining Individual and Familial Therapeutic Alliances

It is essential that the therapist establish and maintain therapeutic alliances with each individual family member and with the family group and subgroups. These alliances are the foundations upon which therapeutic change is built.

#### *Individual Alliances*

The therapist establishes individual alliances by: (1) relating to individual family members as separate, differentiated individuals who are more than just "parts" of the family "whole"; (2) relating to each family member with empathy, respect, concern, and genuineness; and (3) validating the legitimacy of each family member's feelings and thoughts, even though these feelings and thoughts may sometimes conflict.

The process of establishing individual alliances is greatly facilitated by the use of individual interviews. These interviews promote the development of individual alliances by reducing family members' anxieties and by stimulating in them a feeling that the therapist "understands and cares about me as an individual, not just as a member of my family."

*Family Alliances*

The therapist establishes family alliances by: (1) relating to the family or family subsystem as a unit that is more than the sum of its parts; (2) emphasizing the collaborative nature of family problem solving (e.g., "Each of you needs to make some changes in order for the problems in the family to change for the better"); (3) balancing his or her interventions so that he or she remains equally allied with each family member (This does not preclude temporary imbalances, but these should be corrected as soon as possible.); and (4) focusing on those problems and issues that the family wishes to focus on, rather than imposing the therapist's agenda on the family (e.g., by insisting that the "real" problem is the marriage when the parents want to discuss their son's misbehavior).

Conjoint interviews are the essential contexts in which family alliances are developed. It is only by meeting with the family or family subsystem as a group that the therapist can establish a therapeutic alliance with that group.

## Integrating Individual and Family Therapy Techniques

Individual and family alliances provide a framework for integrating individual and family therapy techniques. This integration can take a number of different forms: (1) individually oriented techniques can be used primarily in individual interviews, while family-oriented techniques are used primarily in conjoint family interviews; (2) individually oriented techniques can be combined with family-oriented techniques in conjoint family interviews; and (3) family-oriented techniques can be combined with individually oriented techniques in individual interviews. In the following sections, each of these forms of integration will be discussed.

## Integrating Individually Oriented Techniques Used in Individual Interviews With Family-Oriented Techniques Used in Family Interviews

In many instances, especially when the structure of the therapy is a symmetrical one, individually oriented techniques are used predominantly in individual interviews and family-oriented techniques are used predominantly in family interviews. When this is the case, each type of technique exerts direct effects in the interview format in which it is most extensively utilized and indirect effects in the format in which it is less often utilized. This process is extensively illustrated by the clinical examples presented in the last part of Chapter 4.

## Integrating Individual and Family Therapy Techniques in Conjoint Family and Family Subgroup Interviews

### *Joining the Family via Mutual Empathy and Validation*

The process of joining the family is based on the therapist's empathic listening and empathic responding. As each family member presents his or her view of the family problems, the therapist focuses his or her listening on two levels simultaneously. At the interpersonal level, the focus is on identification of problem-stimulating and problem-reinforcing interactional patterns. At the intrapsychic level, the focus is on empathic understanding of each individual's feelings and thoughts about the presenting problems. Empathic understanding provides a framework for empathic responding. When the therapist's responses reflect an accurate understanding of each person's intrapsychic reactions to the family's interactional problems, these responses facilitate his or her joining with the family in a collaborative effort to change their dysfunctional interactional patterns.

Another critical element in the joining process is validation by the therapist of some aspects of each family member's feelings and thoughts about their interactions. At the individual level, validations facilitate joining by communicating the therapist's acceptance and affirmation of each family member. At the interpersonal level, they establish a framework for viewing the family interactional problems as multidetermined, with each family member playing some role in their etiology and maintenance. To foster therapeutic balance, validations should be spread equally among the various family members.

### Family Restructuring via Mutual Confrontation and Interpretation

Confrontations promote interactional change by stimulating family members to examine those aspects of their behavior and their intrapsychic reactions to other family members' behavior that are contributing to the family's problems. As with validations, it is important that the therapist spread confrontations evenly among the family members, so that no one person feels singled out as the cause of the family problems.

Interpretations of family members' behavior or subjective experience are useful in two ways. For the person to whom the interpretation is made, there is an increase in self-understanding. For the other family members, there is an increase in their understanding of the person to whom the interpretation is made. Often, interpretations are made to more than one family member at the same time. For example, a conflictual couple received the following interpretation, "I think that part of the reason you're both feeling so angry right now is that you've each said or done things that touch a tender nerve in the other. Gloria, when you feel neglected by Bill, it stirs up your feelings of having been neglected by your father. Bill, when you feel criticized by Gloria, it stirs up your feelings of having been harshly criticized by your mother. I believe that each of your current reactions are partly based on these earlier experiences."

When such interpretations are made, it is essential to clarify that while family members' intrapsychic dynamics play an important role in their subjective reactions to each other's behaviors, the behaviors themselves play an equally important role. People may be overreacting to the behaviors of others, but the behaviors to which they are reacting are real and need to change. Each level, the behavioral and the intrapsychic, is equally significant and change at each level is equally important.

*Promoting Effective Family Problem Solving via Emotional and Cognitive Monitoring and Restructuring*

In order for family members to change dysfunctional conflicts into effective problem-solving interactions, they need to learn to monitor and change their emotional and cognitive reactions to one another's behavior. The therapist explains the importance of each person taking responsibility for increasing his or her awareness of the feelings and thoughts experienced during the course of dysfunctional interactions, especially during the earliest stages of such interactions. Family members are then asked to monitor their emotional and cognitive reactions to one another and to identify those reactions that are interfering with constructive problem solving. They are then helped to inhibit or interrupt dysfunctional reactions and to develop more constructive ones via the use of positive coping statements.

*Clinical Illustration*

A couple came for therapy because of dysfunctional conflicts, some of which were characterized by physical violence. In the initial interview, each spouse was asked to take responsibility for monitoring his or her anger and for calling a time-out if he or she felt him- or herself getting more than mildly angry. During the time-out period, they were to practice using anger-management cognitions (Novaco, 1975) to regain emotional control. When they felt they were in control, they were then to try again to discuss their differences in a constructive way. If they started to lose control again, they were to repeat the time-out/cognitive rehearsal procedure.

## Integrating Individual and Family Therapy Techniques in Individual Interviews

### Asking Systemic Questions

As noted in Chapter 1, individual symptoms are stimulated and reinforced, in part, by dysfunctional family interactions. In individual interviews, the therapist can explore the nature of these interactions by asking questions about the interpersonal sequences that precede and follow symptomatic experiences or behaviors (Wachtel & Wachtel, 1986). This process is illustrated by the following examples: (1) A depressed woman was asked about the climate in her marriage during the weeks prior to the onset of her most recent depression. In responding, she initially focused on her husband's current behavior, which was supportive and nurturing. However, she then remembered that during the weeks leading up to the depression he had been quite critical of and demeaning toward her; (2) A husband whose marriage was highly conflictual was asked about the events leading up to the most recent conflict between him and his wife. As he focused on these events, it became clear to him that it was primarily his wife's nonverbal behavior (tone of voice, body posture, etc.) that was hurtful to him, not the verbal content of what she had said; (3) A 10-year-old, school-phobic girl was asked what she did when she stayed home from school. She said that she mostly talked and played games with her mother and that she enjoyed these activities a great deal. Not surprisingly, she preferred staying home with her mother to going to school.

In addition to asking questions that highlight an individual family member's reactions to other family members' behavior, the therapist also asks questions that focus on the reactions of other family members to that individual's behavior. For example, a wife complained that her husband never listened to her when she talked to him. She cited as an example a recent incident when she "told him what a total slob he was; he paid no attention whatsoever." She was asked to think about what his emotional reaction had been to what she had said to him. After some initial resistance ("how should I know what his reaction was?"), she was able to reflect on the question. As she did so, she began to realize that her global criticism had probably evoked feelings of humiliation and anger in her husband and that these feelings were contributing to his failure to listen to her.

## Making Systemic Interpretations

Systemic interpretations, like systemic questions, focus on an individual's subjective reactions to actual or imagined family interactions and/or on other family members' subjective reactions to his or her interactional behavior. Such interpretations may relate to current, past, or future interactions. These different types of interpretation will be illustrated by the following examples, drawn from the therapy of the above-described depressed wife ("Mary") and her husband ("Ted").

*Current interactions.* After exploring Mary's conscious feelings and thoughts about the events leading up to her depressive episode, the following interpretation was made: "I think that when Ted began to be critical of you for not paying enough attention to him, you started to feel guilty, ashamed, and then depressed. As you did so, you began to withdraw from him, which made him feel even more neglected, and led to more criticism from him. It's a real vicious circle."

*Past interactions.* In addition to Mary's feelings and thoughts about her relationship with Ted, her feelings and thoughts about her relationships with the members of her family of origin were also explored. This led to an interpretation linking the two sets of intrapsychic reactions: "I think that part of why you react to Ted's criticisms with guilt and shame is that those criticisms touch off painful feelings about the criticism you so often got from your father."

*Future interactions.* As therapy progressed with Mary and Ted, it became clear that Mary's depression was being maintained, in part, by preconscious anxiety about what might happen if she were to stop being depressed. This anxiety was addressed by the following interpretation: "I think there is a part of you that is afraid that if you were not depressed, Ted would leave you."

## Giving Systemic Suggestions

Behavioral suggestions are most likely to be helpful when the therapist takes into account not only the individual to whom the suggestion is being made but also the family system that forms the context for that individual's behavior. By keeping the systemic context clearly in mind, the therapist is able to suggest specific behavioral changes to help individuals alter the dysfunctional interactional patterns that are contributing to their emotional or behavioral problems. For example: Mary received the suggestion that instead of withdrawing from Ted, she talk with him about how hurtful his criticisms were. She also received a suggestion to explain to him how painful it had been for her to be criticized by her father during childhood. At the same time, Ted received the suggestion that instead of criticizing Mary for withdrawing from him, he ask her to be more aware of his presence and to interact more with him. He also was told that responding positively to Mary when she was not withdrawn was the best way for him to encourage her to increase her involvement with him.

## Using Behavior Rehearsal

Individual interviews are extremely useful contexts for helping family members practice new interactional behaviors. The privacy of the individual interview helps to reduce defensiveness and increases the individual's willingness to try out new ways of behaving. When some degree of mastery has been obtained in the individual interview, these new behaviors can be tried out in the more anxiety-producing context of a conjoint family interview.

## CONCLUSION

Integrated use of individual and family therapy techniques allows the therapist to take advantage of the unique benefits of each type of technique and of the synergistic interactions between them. In an effective integration, each type of technique facilitates and strengthens the therapeutic effects of the other.

# 6

*Potential Problems and How to Deal With Them*

DURING THE COURSE of individual and family therapy integration, a number of problematic situations may arise that have the potential to interfere with therapeutic effectiveness. In this chapter, the most frequent of these potential problems will be described, along with suggested ways of dealing with them.

## RESISTANCE TO INDIVIDUAL OR FAMILY
## INTERVIEWS

### Family Members' Resistance

One problem that the therapist may encounter is the expression of strong resistance to either individual or family interviews by one or more family members. In some instances, the entire family is resistant. In others, the resistance is limited to a family subgroup or a single family member.

In dealing with either of these situations, the first step is exploration of the reasons for the resistance. Sometimes, the resistant family member does not understand the purposes of the resisted format. When this is the case, a clear explanation of those purposes may lead to a decrease in the resistance. In other instances, the resistance may be derived from conscious or unconscious anxiety about what might take place in the resisted format. Here, the therapist needs to empathically explore the nature of the anxiety and the expectations, fantasies, and beliefs that are associated with it. Explanations aimed at changing unrealistic expectations or beliefs are then given. The combination of empathic responsiveness and rational explanation often leads to a reduction in anxiety-based resistance.

## Case Illustration

A wife expressed resistance to coming for an individual assessment interview because she was afraid that if she did so her individual problems, for which she had been receiving individual therapy for a number of years, would become the primary focus of the marital therapy and she would be labeled "the cause" of the marital problems. After some exploration of these feelings, it became clear that her anxiety was derived, in part, from her experiences in her family of origin, where she had consistently been labeled by her parents as "the cause" of the family conflicts. An explanation about the importance of individual assessment interviews for both her and her husband was given, along with assurances that she would not be "blamed" for their marital problems. She did agree to the individual interview, and this interview proved to be an essential part of the assessment process.

At times, the resistance is related to negative experiences with the resisted format in a previous therapy. When this is the case, the most effective strategy is to discuss the specific problems that arose in the previous therapy and then give a clear explanation of what steps will be taken to avoid those problems in the present therapy.

With some families, exploration and explanation are sufficient to reduce resistance to individual or family interviews. With other families, however, the resistances are too strong to be reduced by these measures, at least initially. When this is the case, the resistances need to be a central consideration in the structuring of the therapy.

When the family is united in its resistance to either individual or family interviews, it is usually best to structure the therapy in an asymmetrical way, with the greatest emphasis placed on the least resisted format. In doing this, however, it is important to retain some access to the resisted format. As a general rule of thumb, at least one in four therapy meetings should be in this format. When the frequency is less than that, the resisted format does not occur often enough to exert a substantial effect on the course of the therapy. Also, under those conditions there is not sufficient opportunity for the resistant family members' anxiety about the format to be reduced via desensitization.

With some families, an asymmetrical structure may prove to be effective. With other families, however, the infrequency of the resisted format interferes with the progress of the therapy. In these instances, the therapy needs to shift toward a more symmetrical structure. The most effective way for the therapist to facilitate such a shift is to point out how the resisted format could be helpful in resolving problems in the therapy. This process is illustrated by the following clinical example.

## Case Illustration

A couple came for marital therapy because of increasingly frequent and intense marital conflicts. Initially, both spouses were resistant to individual interviews because they felt that the problems were between the two of them and therefore meeting separately would be a waste of time. The therapist explained the value of integrating individual and conjoint interviews but agreed to limit the individual interviews to once a month. After two months of meeting in this asymmetrical structure, it was clear that the spouses were not making effective use of the conjoint interviews because their anxieties and cognitive distortions were interfering with effective problem solving.

At that point, the therapist suggested a shift to a more symmetrical structure, with the following rationale: "I think the reason that your relationship hasn't changed is that we're not meeting often enough individually. An important part of why you are continuing to have problems is that each of you is reacting internally to the other person's behavior in ways that are interfering with constructive problem solving. For example, some of your reactions, Charlie, when you feel that Alice has been ignoring you and some of your reactions, Alice, when you feel that Charlie has been criticizing you, are blocking you from resolving your differences. In my experience, the work of changing those reactions is most effectively done in individual interviews."

When one or more family members are strongly resistant to individual or family interviews but other family members are not, the situation is more complicated. In some instances, the nonresistant family members are relatively neutral about the therapy structure; they do not express strong positive or negative feelings about either type of meeting. When that is the case, an asymmetrical structure with the most acceptable format predominating is usually the best recommendation.

A more difficult problem arises when one or more family members are resistant to either individual or family interviews while one or more other family members have strong positive feelings about that particular format. For example, a husband may feel that individual interviews are a waste of time, while his wife feels they are extremely valuable. Similarly, the parents of a symptomatic child may not see any reason for conjoint family interviews, while their child feels they are the only safe place for him to talk with his parents about his feelings. In dealing with this problem, the therapist must balance the conflicting feelings of the different family members.

An approach which is often effective is to recommend a symmetrical structure for a limited period of time, making a commitment to deal with the problems raised by the resistant family member. For instance, the therapist might say, "Joe, you feel the individual meetings are a waste of time; Mary, you find them very helpful. I believe that individual meetings are needed, but I'm concerned that you aren't finding them helpful, Joe. My suggestion is that we continue with the individual meetings, at least for a while, but with the understanding that I will explore with you how to make them more meaningful and helpful." If the resistance continues, it may be necessary to cut back on the resisted format. When this is done, it is usually a good idea to suggest that if the family member who feels positively about this format continues to feel the same way, a more symmetrical structure will again be tried.

With couples in which one spouse is overtly symptomatic and the other is not, individual interviews may be strongly resisted by the nonsymptomatic spouse and strongly desired by the symptomatic spouse. In these cases, it is usually best to begin by scheduling conjoint meetings with the couple, individual meetings with the symptomatic spouse as often as necessary, and individual meetings with the nonsymptomatic spouse as often as he or she will tolerate. The meetings with the nonsymptomatic spouse are important because (1) he or she provides a perspective on the symptomatic spouse and on the marriage that is uniquely valuable; (2) he or she may be consciously or unconsciously stimulating and/or reinforcing the partner's symptoms; and (3) he or she may develop symptoms as the other spouse becomes less symptomatic.

At times, all family members may verbally agree to an integrated structure, but one or more of them may subsequently exhibit nonverbal resistance by failing to adhere to the agreed-upon structure. For example, a couple may be scheduled for a conjoint appointment but only one spouse shows up. Similarly, a child may be scheduled for an individual appointment but the parents decide to come instead. In these instances, it is helpful to explain to the family members who are present that it is important to maintain the agreed-upon structure and that if they wish to change the structure for a particular day, it is essential to call and discuss this with the therapist first. Then, the family member who is not present is contacted by telephone and arrangements are made to reschedule as soon as possible. For the remainder of the appointment, the therapist meets with those family members who are present and works on whatever issues they wish to work on.

In some instances, there is no resistance to coming for individual or family meetings but great resistance to using these meetings productively. For example, a spouse may come religiously for individual meetings but in those meetings do nothing but complain about the other spouse's behavior. By the same token, some families come for every conjoint meeting but never discuss anything directly with one another. When faced with this type of resistance, the best approach is to explain the specific benefits of each format, to repeatedly encourage family members to use the resisted format in the most productive way, and to reinforce constructive participation when it occurs.

## Therapist's Resistance

In addition to dealing with one or more family members' resistance to individual or family interviews, the therapist may also have to deal with his or her own resistance to one of these formats. When initial training has been primarily in either individual or family therapy, a therapist is likely to have developed conscious and unconscious resistances to the other way of working. One component of this resistance is anxiety about using a less familiar modality. The other component is biased perception of the more familiar modality as more effective, efficient, or ethical than the less familiar one.

In attempting to integrate individual and family therapy, it is important that the therapist be aware of possible resistances and take effective action to prevent them from interfering with the course of treatment. The first step is to closely examine his or her own feelings and thoughts about each modality and to identify any conscious resistances to the less familiar way of working. The second step is to examine his or her therapeutic behavior for any evidence of unconscious resistance. The most frequent manifestation of such resistance is a pattern of repeatedly recommending asymmetrical therapeutic structures, with the predominating format being the one in which the therapist received primary training.

The therapist's efforts to identify and modify his or her conscious and unconscious resistances can be greatly facilitated by consultation with someone who is highly experienced with both individual and family therapy and with their integration. When the therapist is just starting to work in an integrated way, regular consultation, on a weekly or biweekly basis, is most helpful. Later, consultation on an ad hoc basis is likely to suffice.

## CONFIDENTIALITY

### The Therapist's Confidentiality

As mentioned in Chapter 2, the most important way to avoid problems with confidentiality is for the therapist to clearly explain at the beginning of the assessment process how this issue will be dealt with and to maintain a consistent approach throughout the course of the therapy. However, even when this is done, potential problems sometimes arise.

To maintain confidentiality, it is essential that the therapist be able to distinguish in his or her memory between information that was revealed in a previous individual interview and that which was revealed in a previous conjoint interview. Sometimes, this is not easy to do. The best way to deal with this potential problem is for the therapist to limit his or her comments during conjoint interviews to observations of here-and-now process or to information that he or she is absolutely certain was previously discussed in a conjoint interview. If there is any question about the origin of the information, the therapist should refrain from saying anything about it during the conjoint interview.

At times, the therapist may wish to discuss with one or more family members something that was brought up in an individual interview. It is essential that the therapist not do this without receiving explicit permission from the individual. When the therapist gives a clear explanation of the reasons for the request, most individuals readily grant such permission.

Asking for permission to disclose information to other family members is something that should be done only in an individual meeting. If the therapist asks for such permission during a conjoint meeting, the request itself is a breach of confidentiality. This can create serious problems in the therapist's alliance with the individual family member and with the other family members who are present in the conjoint meeting.

In making a request for permission to disclose, the therapist needs to be specific about what it is that he or she wishes to discuss with other family members. Then the therapist must be careful not to discuss any more than that. When the permission is global rather than specific, for example, "You can tell him about pretty much anything that we've talked about," problems can arise.

*Clinical Illustration*

A student therapist was given this type of global permission by a wife who was separated from her husband. The therapist then met with the husband, sharing with him many things that the wife had said about him during her individual meetings. When the husband heard about the wife's comments, he became enraged with the wife. The wife, in turn, became enraged with the therapist for having told her husband what she had said. When the therapist reminded her of the permission she had given him, she responded, "I didn't mean it was okay for you to tell him about **that!**"

Sometimes, the information that the therapist wishes to disclose has to do with something that is not known to other family members. More often, it has to do with information that is known to other family members but may not be brought up by them in either an individual or family subgroup interview. For example, when one family member discusses a conflict between him or her and one or more other family members, it is important that the therapist be able to discuss this conflict with the other family members who were involved. Since these other family members may or may not bring up the conflict on their own during their next individual or subgroup interview, it is essential that the therapist obtain permission to bring it up. Similarly, when one family member describes another family member as suicidal, it is imperative that the therapist ask permission to discuss this with the other family member who may be too embarrassed, guilty, or self-destructive to raise it.

In the rare instances when an individual is unwilling to permit disclosure, the therapist needs to thoroughly explore the reasons for the reluctance. This exploration occasionally convinces the therapist that disclosure is not, in fact, necessary. More often, the therapist still believes that discussion with other family members is needed. When this is the case, a detailed explanation of the reasons for this belief needs to be given, including the ways in which disclosure will facilitate therapeutic progress and the ways in which lack of disclosure will interfere with such progress. If this explanation is insufficient to convince the individual to give permission for disclosure, the therapist either agrees to proceed without the disclosure or insists on disclosure as a condition for continuation of the therapy. If the therapist chooses the former option, he or she makes clear that the agreement to proceed without disclosure is being made on a trial basis. If it turns out that the lack of disclosure is, in fact, blocking the therapeutic process, the therapist will again raise the issue for discussion.

In extreme instances, the therapist needs to insist on disclosure. One indication for such insistence, previously discussed in Chapter 2, is the therapist's belief that lack of disclosure would endanger the health or safety of the individual with whom he or she is meeting or of one or more other individuals.

A second indication is the therapist's belief that without disclosure he or she would not be able to conduct the therapy in an ethical way. Most commonly, this issue arises when one family member discusses something with the therapist that he or she has kept secret from the other family members. If the therapist believes that it would be unethical to continue the therapy unless the secret is disclosed, he or she needs to insist on disclosure. An example of this type of situation is the couple described in Chapter 2. The husband's business was in serious financial trouble, and he was afraid to reveal this fact to his wife. The therapist insisted on disclosure because he felt it would be unethical to proceed without the wife being apprised of her financial situation.

Sometimes, when the therapist learns about something that is being kept secret from other family members, he or she can suggest that the individual either disclose the secret or stop the behavior that is being kept secret. For example, if a spouse reveals that he or she is currently having an extramarital affair, the therapist can suggest that either the affair be disclosed or that it be stopped.

## Family Members' Confidentiality

A different type of problem with confidentiality can arise when family members discuss their individual interviews with each other. In reporting the therapist's comments, family members may consciously or unconsciously slant or distort what was said. One family member may say to another, for instance, that the therapist "thinks our problems are your fault." The individual's reactions to such a statement can seriously threaten the therapist's alliance with that person.

This problem can usually be avoided if the therapist makes clear to all family members from the outset that, while they are free to discuss their individual interviews with each other if they wish to do so, it is essential that they talk with the therapist about any confusion, hurt feelings, disappointment, or anger that may arise from these discussions. When a family member does talk with the therapist about something the therapist reportedly said, the therapist needs to clarify what, in fact, was said and discuss any misunderstandings. This must be done with whoever is bringing the issue to the therapist's attention and with the family member who originally reported the therapist's remarks. It is important for the therapist not to be judgmental or blaming toward the family member who misrepresented his or her comments. It is best to assume that the misrepresentation was the result of misunderstanding, not malice, and that the therapist may have been partly responsible for the misunderstanding. In this way, the therapist models the type of approach to conflict that he or she is trying to help the family members develop in their interactions with each other.

## LACK OF SYSTEMATIC TREATMENT PLANNING

When therapists begin to integrate individual and family therapy, they often make the mistake of prescribing the same structure (e.g., symmetrical integration) for all families, rather than systematically planning, in conjunction with the family, an approach that is congruent with that family's particular problems, strengths, and resistances. Some families need a symmetrical structure; others are more likely to benefit from a predominantly individual or conjoint structure. Also, while many individuals and families are highly receptive to a symmetrical structure, others are so resistant to either individual or conjoint interviews that an asymmetrical structure is the only one they will accept, at least initially. When the therapist does not plan the therapy to fit the particular needs and resistances of the specific individuals and families, the likelihood of therapeutic success is greatly diminished.

An equally common mistake that therapists are prone to make when they first begin to integrate individual and family therapy is automatic acceptance of the family's expectations regarding therapeutic structure. While it is important to take the family's expectations into account, many families are open to changing their expectations if given a clear explanation of why the therapist is recommending a therapeutic structure different from what they were expecting. For example, the parents of a symptomatic child may be expecting individual therapy for their youngster but readily agree to an integration of individual and conjoint family meetings when the therapist explains the value of conjoint discussions of family interactional problems. Conversely, a couple may arrive expecting conjoint meetings only but agree to individual meetings as well when the therapist explains the value of talking with each person separately about that person's feelings and thoughts about the marriage and about him- or herself.

## OTHER CURRENT THERAPIES

In some instances, one or more family members are currently engaged in another psychotherapy. With couples, one or both spouses may be in individual or group therapy. With families, one or both parents may be in individual or group therapy or the parental couple may be in marital therapy. When this is the case, it is important to invite those family members who are currently in another therapy to discuss with the therapist any differences in approach or interpretation that may arise. On occasion, direct contact with the other therapist may be helpful. If this is done, permission from all participating family members must be obtained.

The fact that one or more family members are in concurrent individual, group, or marital therapy should be taken into account in formulating an integrative treatment plan, but it should not be the major determinant of that plan. For instance, if the therapist believes that a couple needs an individually oriented structure in order to resolve their marital problems, this structure should be recommended, regardless of whether one or both spouses is concurrently in individual therapy.

## LACK OF THERAPEUTIC BALANCE

As discussed in Chapter 5, it is extremely important that the therapist establish and maintain balance in his or her interactions with the different family members. When the therapist does not do so, serious problems often arise.

With couples, the therapy may become unbalanced when the therapist identifies (consciously or unconsciously) with one spouse more than the other. This identification may be based on demographic characteristics, such as age or sex, or it may be based on personality style. For instance, the therapist may identify with one spouse's verbal aggressiveness, conflict-avoidance, autonomy, or dependency. Overidentification with one spouse is usually manifested by excessive validation and inadequate confrontation of that spouse by the therapist.

The therapist may also lose therapeutic balance when he or she has a conscious or unconscious aversive reaction to one of the spouses. Again, this reaction may be triggered by demographic characteristics or personality style. When the therapist has such a negative reaction to one of the spouses, he or she is most likely to be inadequately validating and excessively confrontational toward that spouse.

Whether the imbalance is based on overidentification with or aversion to one of the spouses, it disrupts the even-handed relatedness that is essential for effective therapeutic work with couples. The spouse with whom the therapist is overidentified is likely to be less motivated to work on his or her contribution to the marital problems. In this case, the spouse will experience the therapist as an ally and his or her contribution to the marital problems will be less well delineated. The spouse with whom the therapist is less identified or toward whom the therapist has an aversive reaction is likely to feel frustrated, hurt, and angry about the therapist's "abandonment" of him or her in favor of the other. In some instances, this spouse may react with feelings of worthlessness and hopelessness ("It's all my fault—even my therapist thinks so").

With families, therapeutic balance is most often lost when the therapist overidentifies either with a symptomatic child or adolescent or with the parents. The first type of overidentification interferes with the development of a therapeutic alliance between the therapist and the parents. Without such an alliance, the parents will resist participating in the therapy and will resist their child's participation. At times, they may abruptly terminate the therapy. When the therapist overidentifies with the parents, the necessary alliance between the therapist and the symptomatic child or adolescent will not develop. Without this alliance, effective therapeutic work between the therapist and child is impossible.

As with couples, therapeutic balance may also be lost because the therapist reacts aversively to either the symptomatic child or the parents. This can lead to excessive confrontation or inadequate validation of one or the other.

The most effective way for the therapist to deal with therapeutic imbalances is to prevent them from occurring in the first place. In order to do this, it is essential that the therapist be closely attuned to his or her emotional and cognitive reactions to each family member. When he or she becomes aware of any imbalances in positive or negative reactions to the various family members, these reactions need to be fully understood and changed, as quickly as possible.

A therapist's overidentifications and aversive reactions are often derived from unresolved conscious or unconscious conflicts in relation to the members of his or her family of origin and/or present family (i.e., they are countertransference reactions). For this reason, it is important for the therapist to resolve as many such conflicts as possible and to be as clear as possible about those conflicts that remain unresolved. Personal psychotherapy (individual, family, or both) and case consultation are both likely to prove helpful in this effort.

In addition to working on unresolved conflicts, the therapist can work directly on changing his or her perceptions of the various family members. When there is an overidentification with one family member, the therapist needs to focus on the ways that this family member is contributing to the problems between him or her and other family members. When there is an aversive reaction to one family member, the therapist needs to focus on the strengths of this family member and the positive contributions that he or she is making to the overall well-being of the family.

Individual interviews are especially useful for this purpose. In an individual interview, the therapist can concentrate on his or her reactions to that particular individual without being distracted by the interactions between that person and other family members. Later, he or she can continue to work on changing his or her reactions in the more complex setting of a conjoint interview.

**Clinical Illustrations**

(1) A therapist brought a case for consultation in which he was feeling frustrated about his inability to "get anywhere" with the husband in a couple that he was seeing for marital problems. The husband had great difficulty expressing his feelings and resisted coming for individual interviews. The therapist felt frustrated and angry with him and was at a loss about how to overcome the husband's resistance. As the therapist examined his reactions to this man, he became aware of a connection between his feelings toward him and his feelings toward his father, who had been emotionally unexpressive, cold, and distant. Awareness of this connection helped him to gain a clearer perspective on his reactions to the husband and to focus on the ways in which the husband was cooperating in the therapy and in the marriage. Over time, the therapist began to react more positively toward the husband and discovered ways to help him overcome his resistance to emotional expressiveness.

(2) Another therapist came for consultation about a family that she was seeing because of conflict between the 10-year-old daughter and the mother. The daughter was described by her mother as angry, defiant, and disrespectful. The daughter described her mother as unreasonably demanding and rigid. The therapist found herself identifying with the daughter and repeatedly felt inclined to take her side in her disputes with the mother. As the therapist's reactions were examined, it became clear that her identification with the daughter was derived, in part, from her

feelings about the chronic conflict between her and her mother while she was growing up. As she explored these connections, she began to see that the daughter was often disrespectful toward her mother and often overreacted to her mother's reasonable restrictions. These realizations helped the therapist to regain a more balanced position in her therapeutic interactions with mother and daughter.

## LACK OF FEEDBACK FROM FAMILY MEMBERS

The establishment and maintenance of effective therapeutic alliances are greatly facilitated when the therapist elicits feedback from the family members about their experience of the structure and process of the therapy. Initially, a request for feedback is made during the assessment phase when a treatment plan is being made. At that time, family members' reactions to the individual and conjoint assessment interviews are a major factor in the development of the treatment plan.

When the treatment plan begins to be implemented, it is helpful to request that family members discuss with the therapist any negative reactions that they may have to either the therapeutic structure or process. This explicit request often facilitates the giving of feedback from individuals who otherwise would be too frightened, embarrassed, or guilty to do so.

When the therapist does not receive explicit feedback from family members, he or she will often misread their reactions to the treatment plan and/or the therapeutic process. This can lead to frustrating therapeutic stalemates or premature termination. When the therapist does receive such feedback, his or her ability to accurately assess the state of the therapeutic alliance with each family member is greatly enhanced. This, in turn, enhances the likelihood of therapeutic success.

## ANTICIPATING AND PREVENTING PROBLEMS

When the therapist is aware of the potential problems that may develop during the course of individual and family therapy integration, he or she is in a position to anticipate and prevent their occurrence. The therapist's preventive efforts begin at the outset of therapy and continue through each phase of the therapy process. Many of the steps that the therapist can take to prevent the development of problems have been described in the present chapter. Others will be delineated in the following chapter, which focuses on the phases of individual and family therapy integration.

# 7

*Phases of Individual and Family Therapy Integration*

INDIVIDUAL AND family therapy integration proceeds through a series of phases. Each phase is characterized by a specific set of goals, methods for promoting the achievement of those goals, potential problems that may interfere with goal attainment, and methods for avoiding or overcoming such problems. In this chapter, the characteristic goals, problems, and methods of each phase of the therapeutic process will be described.

## FIRST PHASE

The first phase of individual and family therapy integration is directed toward (1) establishing rapport with each family member and with the family group and subgroups; (2) conducting a comprehensive, multilevel assessment of individual and family interactional problems and strengths; and (3) establishing a mutually acceptable integrative treatment plan. The first two goals are pursued simultaneously from the outset. The third goal is based on successful attainment of the first two.

## Rapport

The most important initial goal is the establishment of rapport. When family members feel that the therapist cares about, respects, and understands them, they are able to form effective diagnostic and therapeutic alliances.

The therapist establishes rapport with individual family members by relating to each one with respect, concern, and genuineness (Rogers, 1980), by clarifying each person's view of the presenting problems, by communicating empathic understanding of each person's feelings and thoughts, by validating some part of each person's point of view, and by exploring and reinforcing individual strengths and resources. Rapport with the family group and subgroups is established by relating to the group as a unique entity that is more than the sum of its parts, by clarifying areas of agreement and disagreement among the family members, by delineating the ways in which each person's behaviors and subjective reactions are related to those of the others, and by exploring and reinforcing the family's strengths and resources.

Conjoint interviews are particularly valuable contexts for establishing rapport with the family group and subgroups. By meeting with family members together in the same room at the same time, the therapist is able to directly experience their interactional patterns and to establish a relationship with each person within the context of those patterns. Individual interviews are particularly valuable for establishing rapport with individual family members. In these interviews, the therapist is able to directly experience the individual separate from the family and to form a relationship with him or her as a separate person, not just as a member of the family. Integrating conjoint and individual interviews greatly facilitates the establishment of rapport at both the individual and family group levels.

Problems with establishing rapport can occur for a number of reasons. In some instances, the therapist does not take sufficient time to explore each family member's feelings and thoughts, is not empathically attuned to each person's subjective experiences, is more empathically responsive to some family members than to others, or reacts aversively to one or more family members. In other instances, the therapist fails to understand the implicit rules governing family interactions or fails to utilize this understanding to guide his or her interventions. These problems can usually be avoided if the therapist is careful to ensure that each family member is given an opportunity to express his or her feelings and thoughts, listens empathically when each person speaks, actively searches for some elements of each person's point of view that can honestly be validated, and uses his or her understanding of the family rules as a guide for therapeutic intervention.

When problems with rapport do arise, it is helpful for the therapist to carefully examine his or her subjective reactions to the family and to each individual family member. In doing so, he or she may discover feelings and thoughts about one or more family members that had been outside of conscious awareness. After becoming aware of such feelings and thoughts, the therapist examines the connections between these subjective reactions and his or her own family experiences, both in the family of origin and in the current family. At times, consultation can be helpful in analyzing these connections and then using this analysis to help remove the blocks to the establishment of rapport.

## Assessment

At the same time that the therapist is promoting the establishment of rapport, he or she is also assessing the problems and strengths of each family member and of the family group and subgroups. In conjoint interviews, the therapist observes verbal and nonverbal interactional patterns, using these observations to formulate an assessment of the family rules, roles, and homeostatic dynamics. In individual interviews, the therapist empathically assesses individual feelings, thoughts, and behaviors, using this assessment to develop a formulation of conscious and unconscious cognitive and emotional dynamics. Integration of the observations derived from the conjoint and individual interviews enables the therapist to develop a comprehensive, multilevel assessment of individual and family interactional problems and strengths.

Difficulties with assessment can arise when the therapist does not include one or more components of the assessment process (family, family subgroup, and individual interviews), focuses too heavily on either interactional or intrapsychic dynamics, or fails to integrate his or her interactional and intrapsychic formulations.

Failing to include one or more components of the assessment process is usually a result of conscious or unconscious resistance to integrating conjoint and individual interviews. When therapists begin to learn an integrated approach, they typically have more familiarity and comfort with one of these formats than with the other. Their anxiety about using the less familiar format can lead them to leave out this element of the assessment process. For example, a therapist with a primarily individually oriented background may fail to include a conjoint family meeting in the initial assessment process. Conversely, a therapist with a primarily family-oriented background may conduct a conjoint family meeting but fail to meet separately with either the parents or the child.

A related problem is focusing too heavily on either interactional or intrapsychic dynamics. Therapists whose initial training was primarily in family therapy are likely to do the former, while those whose initial training was primarily in individual therapy are likely to do the latter. When either type of imbalance occurs, the resulting assessment will be incomplete and skewed.

Even when the therapist does focus equally on interactional and intrapsychic dynamics, he or she may not focus on the ways in which factors at these two levels influence each other. This leads to separate but unrelated formulations of interactional and intrapsychic dynamics, rather than an integrated, multilevel formulation.

In order to prevent these problems, the therapist needs to be fully aware of his or her anxiety about using relatively unfamiliar concepts. The therapist can utilize this awareness to stimulate constructive action rather than counter-productive resistance. Open discussion with colleagues and supervisors about this type of anxiety and about constructive ways to deal with it can be very helpful in achieving this objective.

### Treatment Planning

Comprehensive, multilevel assessment is followed by comprehensive, multilevel treatment planning. The therapist's treatment recommendations are based on his or her assessment of the individual and family interactional problems, the interpersonal and intrapsychic factors that are stimulating and maintaining those problems, and the individual and familial strengths and resources. These treatment recommendations are discussed with the family members. Based on their reactions, the plan may be implemented in its original form or one or more modifications may be made. In either case, an agreement is made to review the plan within a relatively short period of time after its implementation.

Problems with treatment planning arise when the therapist's recommendations are based on an incomplete or inaccurate assessment, when the therapist fails to tailor the treatment plan to the particular problems and strengths of specific individuals and families, or when he or she fails to collaborate with the family members in the development of the final treatment plan.

Incomplete assessment has been discussed in the preceding section. Treatment recommendations based on such an assessment fail to take into account all of the important factors that are contributing to the maintenance of the presenting problems. They also fail to take into account all of the individual and familial strengths and resources that provide a basis for problem resolution. Therefore, those recommendations are not likely to lead to successful therapy.

Lack of specificity in treatment planning is most often a result of rigid application of one form of integration—symmetrical or asymmetrical—to all cases. In some instances, this happens because the therapist is inclined to recommend the structure making the greatest use of the format he or she is most familiar with. For example, a therapist whose background is primarily in individual therapy may tend to recommend individually oriented integration, while a therapist whose background is primarily in family therapy may tend to recommend family-oriented integration. In other instances, the therapist recommends symmetrical integration all the time, incorrectly assuming that because this structure makes equal use of both formats, it is always the most effective way of working. Neither of these approaches is productive. The therapist needs to be equally comfortable using any of the different forms of individual and family therapy integration and needs to tailor his or her therapeutic recommendations to the particular therapeutic needs of specific individuals and families.

When the therapist does develop specific therapeutic recommendations, it is essential that these recommendations be discussed with the family members so that they can express their feelings about them. Such collaboration greatly reduces the risk that one or more family members will undermine the treatment plan in response to feeling excluded from the plan's developmental process.

## SECOND PHASE

The second phase of individual and family therapy integration begins with the implementation of the treatment plan. The major goals of this phase are the reduction or elimination of individual and family interactional problems, the development of effective strategies for preventing the recurrence of those problems, and the enhancement of individual and familial strengths and resources. The therapist pursues these goals by stimulating and integrating intrapsychic and behavioral change processes.

### Implementation and Monitoring of the Treatment Plan

As the initial treatment plan is put into practice, the therapist focuses on two tasks simultaneously. The first task is the implementation of the treatment plan. The second is ongoing evaluation of the effectiveness of that plan. This evaluation is based on the therapist's observations of family members' behavior during therapy sessions, family members' descriptions of their behavior outside of therapy sessions, and family members' subjective reactions to the structure and process of the therapy. The therapist's understanding of the latter is greatly enhanced by explicitly asking family members about their reactions to the therapy. It is helpful for the therapist to ask about these reactions in both conjoint and individual interviews.

Not uncommonly, one or more family members will discuss feelings and thoughts about the therapy in an individual interview that he or she would not be able or willing to discuss in a conjoint family interview. Conversely, the context of a conjoint interview often stimulates discussion of feelings and thoughts about the therapy that would not have been brought up in an individual interview.

The therapist combines the family members' feedback with his or her own observations about how the existing therapeutic plan is working. He or she then recommends either continuing with the existing plan or making one or more modifications. These recommendations are discussed with the family members and a collaborative decision is made about how to proceed.

The structure and process of the therapy are periodically evaluated in this way throughout the course of treatment. This creates a climate in which therapeutic goals are kept clearly in focus, explicit decisions are made about the best ways to achieve those goals, and a spirit of collaborative problem solving is developed.

If the therapist does not monitor the therapeutic process, he or she will not be able to determine whether or not the existing structure is successfully promoting the achievement of the therapeutic objectives. If the therapist is not aware of family members' feelings and thoughts about the therapy, his or her ability to sustain effective therapeutic alliances will be impaired. Under these circumstances, it is not uncommon for the therapy to wander aimlessly, like a ship without a rudder, or to abruptly terminate because of one or more family members' negative reactions to either the therapeutic structure or process.

In addition to eliciting and discussing family members' reactions to the therapy, the therapist also needs to be open to responding to those reactions by changing either the therapeutic structure or process. If the therapist rigidly adheres to the initial plan, therapeutic alliances will be weakened and the likelihood of therapeutic success will be diminished. This does not imply, however, that the treatment plan should automatically be changed every time one or more family members voice a negative reaction. Discussion of such reactions may well suggest that the best approach is to stay with the existing structure. The important thing is for the therapist to be open to hearing and discussing family members' reactions to the existing treatment plan and open to changing the plan if it appears that this would enhance the effectiveness of the therapy.

## Clinical Illustrations

(1) Nancy and Fred came for marital therapy because of dysfunctional marital conflict. After the initial assessment, a symmetrical treatment structure was recommended. They accepted this recommendation and treatment began. After about two months, they said that they were getting a lot out of the conjoint appointments but didn't feel the need for so many individual appointments. After discussing these feelings and thoughts with them, the therapist agreed to shift to a conjoint-oriented structure, in which they were seen conjointly two weeks in a row, then each of them was seen individually. This structure worked well and was maintained for the duration of the therapy.

(2) John and Connie came for marital therapy because Connie was unhappy about John's frequent angry outbursts toward her and their children. The initial treatment plan was for a symmetrically integrated therapy. After about a

month, John expressed negative feelings about the individual interviews, saying that he didn't understand how they could help him and Connie get along better. Exploration of these feelings revealed that John was feeling anxious about the individual interviews because he feared that the therapist would blame him for all the problems in the marriage. The therapist explained that he did not view John as "the one to blame" for the marital problems, but he did think that John's lack of control over his anger was contributing to those problems and that individual interviews were necessary to help him overcome his anger dyscontrol. John agreed to continue the symmetrical structure and subsequently made good use of the individual interviews.

(3) Andy and Bonnie sought marital therapy because of lack of intimacy in their relationship. At their request, the initial therapy structure was individually oriented. Each spouse met with the therapist for individual interviews once a week. They met conjointly once a month. This structure worked well for about six months. At that point, the therapist recommended shifting to a symmetrical structure in order to help them develop more effective problem-solving skills. They agreed to this change and the symmetrical structure was maintained for the duration of the therapy.

## Stimulation and Integration of Intrapsychic and Behavioral Change Processes

In pursuing the goals of the second phase of treatment, the therapist stimulates and integrates intrapsychic and behavioral change processes. In a symmetrically integrated therapy, both types of change process receive equal attention. In an asymmetrically integrated therapy, greater attention is given to one than to the other; however, even in an asymmetrical integration, both types of change process are of crucial importance.

Behavioral change processes are most effectively stimulated in the context of conjoint interviews by means of interpersonally oriented techniques. Intrapsychic change processes are most effectively stimulated in the context of individual interviews by means of individually oriented techniques. This does not mean that individually oriented techniques cannot or should not be used in conjoint interviews, nor that interpersonally oriented techniques cannot or should not be used in individual interviews. Indeed, specific methods for using these techniques in these ways have been described in Chapter 5. Nonetheless, there are specific advantages to using interpersonally oriented techniques primarily in conjoint interviews and intrapsychically oriented techniques primarily in individual interviews.

In conjoint interviews, the therapist can intervene directly when dysfunctional interactional patterns are observed, can model more effective ways of interacting, and can provide a context in which new interactional patterns can be practiced and reinforced. In individual interviews, the therapist can most effectively explore conscious and unconscious emotions and cognitions, can interpret the connections between current reactions and past experiences, and can use role-play modeling and rehearsal to help individuals develop new forms of behavior. By integrating both types of format, the therapist maximizes his or her ability to promote both types of change process.

Therapeutic changes typically occur in stages. Initially, there is often a reduction in the frequency and intensity of the presenting problems. In some cases, these changes are lasting. More often, they are followed by a regression to the initial state; sometimes, the regression leads to a state that is worse than the initial one. This can be discouraging to family members and to the therapist, especially the inexperienced therapist. With experience, therapists learn that such regressions are temporary and do not mean that no "real" change has taken place. What they do mean is that human beings are creatures of habit and that dysfunctional habit patterns resist change. When the therapist understands the nature of this resistance, he or she will be able to make use of it to promote the therapeutic objectives.

Family members resist changing primarily because they are afraid to change. The therapist's job is to help them understand the nature of their fear and develop strategies for reducing it. In conjoint family interviews, the therapist anticipates resistance to behavioral change by asking family members to discuss their feelings and thoughts about making the changes that other family members have asked them to make. In individual and family subgroup interviews, the therapist empathically explores the conscious and preconscious thoughts, images, fantasies, beliefs, and conflicts that underlie family members' resistance-promoting feelings of anxiety.

## Clinical Illustration

Tony, a 15-year-old high school freshman, was brought for therapy by his parents because of his poor grades, refusal to attend all of his classes, refusal to follow through on his chores at home, and belligerent attitude toward his parents and teachers. In a conjoint family interview, Tony asked his parents to "stop criticizing me all the time." They, in turn, asked him to stop his belligerent behavior, attend all his classes, and improve his grades in school. They all agreed to make these behavioral changes, but little change actually took place.

In a separate interview with the parents, their feelings about Tony's request were explored. This revealed that they were afraid that if they ignored any of his belligerent behaviors, no matter how minor, the frequency of those behaviors would increase. Similarly, they were afraid that if they praised him when he behaved appropriately, he would interpret that as permission not to change his inappropriate behaviors. As a result, they continued to criticize him very frequently and to withhold any positive reinforcement.

In an individual interview with Tony, the reasons for his resistance to change were explored. He indicated that he was afraid that if he changed, he would no longer have any friends. He felt that the only reason people wanted to be his friend was that they thought he was "cool" because he didn't follow the rules at school or at home. He feared they would experience him as a "nerd" if he started attending all his classes and getting good grades.

After identifying these resistance-promoting anxieties, the therapist worked with the parents and with Tony to reduce them. He explained to the parents that while their fears were understandable they were, in fact, contrary to what is known about how behavior changes. The parents were then encouraged to ignore minor negative behaviors and reinforce as many positive behaviors as possible. The therapist worked with Tony to help him learn to tolerate his fear of rejection and to develop enough self-confidence to risk making constructive behavioral changes, even though other people might think less of him for doing so. Over time, these strategies were successful in helping Tony increase his prosocial behavior and in helping his parents increase their affirming behavior.

During the course of therapy, the change process is usually characterized by a series of advances and regressions. It is helpful for the therapist to explain that this pattern is typical of human change and that the regressions can be valuable stimuli for learning about the nature of the problems and about those factors that are maintaining the problems. When the frequency and intensity of the regressions have been substantially reduced, the process of therapy shifts to its third, or termination, phase.

### THIRD PHASE

The third phase of individual and family therapy integration is characterized by consolidation and strengthening of the changes that have occurred during the second phase, development of a plan for termination, and implementation of the termination plan. In this section, the process of termination will be discussed in terms of its initiation, structure, and course.

## Initiation

The termination process begins when either one or more family members or the therapist raises the question of whether the time is right to begin making plans to terminate the therapy. In some cases, this question is raised relatively soon after the beginning of therapy. In others, it is brought up after a more lengthy therapeutic course.

When a family member raises the question of termination, the therapist's first task is to explore his or her reasons for raising the question at this time. In this exploration, the therapist looks for both rational and irrational, conscious and unconscious reasons. It is important for the therapist to be balanced in his or her listening so that none of these factors is underestimated. An expressed desire to terminate may be a defense against anxiety. On the other hand, it may be a sign of healthy self-confidence. The therapist's job is to listen for both types of motivation and to assess how much of each is present.

After assessing the feelings and thoughts of the person who raised the question of termination, the therapist explores the reactions of the other family members. Here again, it is important to listen carefully for both defensive and adaptive reactions. The other family members may express feelings and thoughts that are similar to those of the initiating family member, or there may be differences between that person's position and that of one or more other family members. When there are differences, the therapist helps the family to clarify their differences and to discuss them in a constructive way.

After clarifying each family member's feelings and thoughts about termination, the therapist shares his or her own thoughts (and sometimes feelings) about this issue. If there is a consensus among the family members and the therapist agrees with this consensus, a termination plan can be made immediately. If there is not a consensus, or if the therapist disagrees with the consensus that the family members have reached, he or she explains the reasons for his or her position and then works with the family members to reach a mutually acceptable plan of action.

In discussing termination plans, it is important for the therapist to be aware of the possibility that his or her feelings and thoughts about this issue, like those of the family members, may be affected by conscious or unconscious irrational processes. For instance, the therapist may be afraid to reinforce family members' positive feelings about termination because of unconscious guilt feelings about abandoning people who may still need him or her. On the other hand, the therapist may be too quick to reinforce such feelings because of anxiety about people becoming too dependent on him or her. By being alert to these types of reactions, the therapist can reduce the chances that they will influence his or her therapeutic interventions.

When the therapist is the one who raises the question of termination, the process is somewhat different. First of all, it is essential that the therapist carefully explore his or her reasons for wanting to introduce this subject before actually doing so. As before, there are rational and irrational, conscious and unconscious reasons why a therapist might want to initiate discussion of termination. It is the therapist's responsibility to make sure that his or her reasons are rational and adaptive, rather than irrational and defensive.

In general, it is best for the therapist not to introduce

discussion of termination unless there are strong signals from the family members that they are feeling ready to terminate. For instance, they may repeatedly say such things as, "We really don't seem to have much to talk about in here anymore"; "Our problems seem pretty manageable now"; or "Things are much improved." In response to such signals, the therapist may decide to explore the family members' feelings about termination. As before, it is important for the therapist to be alert for both rational and irrational feelings. It is especially important to listen for specific reactions to the fact that it was the therapist who initiated discussion of termination. One or more family members may feel that this action by the therapist means that he or she doesn't like that person or his or her family, is bored, thinks they are hopeless, and so forth. These reactions need to be explored, discussed, and resolved.

Whether it is the therapist or one or more family members who take the initial step, the process of termination planning involves the integrated use of conjoint and individual interviews. Each of these formats has unique and complementary benefits. In conjoint interviews, family members can discuss and clarify their feelings and thoughts about termination, interpersonal conflicts about this issue can be resolved, and a mutually acceptable agreement can be negotiated. In individual interviews, conscious and unconscious feelings and thoughts about termination can be explored, anxieties and conflicts can be reduced, and rational thinking can be enhanced.

## Structure

During the termination phase, the structure of the therapy may remain the same as it was during the last part of the second phase, or it may change one or more times. The most frequent changes are reduction in the frequency of appointments and greater use of combined, rather than sequential, integration.

Reducing the frequency of appointments provides family members (and the therapist) an opportunity to experience, rather than just imagine, their emotional, cognitive, and behavioral reactions to the loss of therapeutic contact. These reactions are often important indicators of issues that need further work prior to stopping the therapy. Of particular importance are issues regarding separation and loss.

Frequency reduction also provides an opportunity for the family to generalize the changes that have occurred in the therapy sessions to their day-to-day life outside of therapy. Generalization greatly increases the likelihood that such changes will persist after all therapy sessions have been stopped.

The frequency of therapy sessions can be reduced in one or more stages. For example, if sessions have been taking place once a week, the first reduction would be to once every other week. Later, there would be a second reduction to once a month. Multiple-stage reduction often facilitates therapeutic generalization because it provides an opportunity for family members to experience increasingly closer approximations to full termination, while continuing to have the therapist available to help them examine their reactions to these experiences.

In addition to reducing the frequency of therapy sessions, it is often helpful to shift from sequential integration to combined integration. For instance, a couple had been coming for weekly therapy appointments, alternating between conjoint and individual interviews in a symmetrical structure. When the frequency of their appointments was reduced to every other week, the structure was changed to a combined one, so that each appointment was divided into conjoint and individual components (e.g., individual appointments with each spouse followed by a conjoint appointment). This allowed the therapist to continue to utilize the strengths of each format even though the frequency of therapy sessions had been reduced.

If the structure of the therapy has been an asymmetrical one, the shift to combined integration takes place within the framework of the asymmetry. For instance, a family had been coming for weekly conjoint family meetings and monthly individual meetings with the child and parents separately. When the frequency of sessions was reduced to every other week, conjoint family meetings alternated with combined individual-parent-family meetings. This structure allowed the therapist to continue to utilize primarily conjoint family meetings, while also continuing to meet separately with the child and parents once a month.

## COURSE

The termination phase may be short, medium, or long. In some cases, it may last only one or two weeks. In others, it may take many months. The length of this phase is determined primarily by the family members' readiness to engage in the termination process, their tolerance for the anxiety inherent in this process, the therapist's ability to facilitate the termination process, and his or her tolerance for the anxiety associated with this phase.

The course of the termination phase may be smooth, with a steady progression toward termination, or it may be characterized by one or more episodes of regression, in which problems that had been present in earlier phases of the therapy reemerge, sometimes more intensely than before. Because of the frequency of such regressions, it is helpful for the therapist to discuss this possibility with the family members prior to the initiation of the termination process. This reduces the likelihood that family members will panic if a regression does occur, and it provides a framework for utilizing the regression as a vehicle for therapeutic work.

When regressions occur, the therapist works with the family members in two ways. First, he or she clarifies each person's feelings and thoughts about the regression, helps them discuss these feelings and thoughts, and then facilitates the renegotiation of behavior-change agreements. Second, the therapist helps the family members understand the connections between their behavioral regression and their subjective, conscious and unconscious anxiety about termination. Conjoint family interviews are particularly helpful contexts in which to do the first type of work; individual interviews are particularly helpful contexts for doing the second type of work.

When the regressions have been worked through, a termination date is set. In the last scheduled interview, it is helpful to review the work that has been done in the therapy, to reinforce the positive changes that each family member has made, and to make a clear plan about the future. It is helpful to indicate that while the therapist believes the family is ready for termination, he or she will be available for consultation if they "get stuck." When families do return for a follow-up appointment, they often need very little help to get themselves unstuck and back on track. In some instances, more extensive additional therapy is needed.

## CONCLUSION

Each phase of individual and family therapy integration is an essential component of the overall process. The first phase is the foundation for each of the other phases. The second phase builds on the first and is the arena in which most therapeutic changes take place. The third phase promotes consolidation and generalization of therapeutic gains and provides important opportunities for growth and development, especially in regard to issues of separation and loss.

# 8

*Conclusion*

INDIVIDUAL AND family therapy integration is part of a larger movement to integrate the psychotherapies (Beitman, Goldfried & Norcross, 1989; Norcross & Goldfried, in press). This movement has four major objectives: (1) to identify common factors among the many different forms of psychotherapy; (2) to identify specific strengths and weaknesses of different therapeutic approaches; (3) to develop ways of integrating different therapeutic approaches so that the complementary benefits of each approach can be utilized to promote therapeutic change; and (4) to tailor the structure and process of psychotherapy to meet the specific therapeutic needs of the individuals or families who are seeking help. In this concluding chapter, these objectives will be utilized as a framework for presenting an overview of the theory and practice of individual and family therapy integration.

## COMMON FACTORS

Individual and family therapy share a number of concepts and therapeutic strategies. Conceptually, both approaches emphasize that dysfunctional behaviors and subjective states are not random events, but rather they can be understood as attempts to cope with internal and/or external reality. Therapeutically, each approach highlights the importance of forming and maintaining therapeutic alliances, of developing a mutually acceptable treatment plan, and of intervening in ways that are congruent with the therapeutic needs and resistances of the individuals or families who are seeking help.

In regard to therapeutic change processes, individual and family therapy seem very different; however, some of the differences between the approaches are more apparent than real. For example, family therapists are often critical of individual therapists for their emphasis on the importance of insight as a therapeutic change process. Instead of insight, these therapists emphasize the importance of "second-order change" processes leading to shifts in fundamental properties of family systems (Watzlawick, Weakland, & Fisch, 1974). The examples used to illustrate the process of second-order change make it clear, however, that insight, defined as increased conscious awareness of current emotional, cognitive, and behavioral reactions, is a major element of this process.

Similarly, individual therapists are often critical of family therapists for their emphasis on behavioral, rather than intrapsychic, change processes. For them, insight and working through are the major vehicles for therapeutic change. However, close examination of the concepts of insight and working through reveals the presence of many behavioral elements (P. L. Wachtel, 1977).

## SPECIFIC STRENGTHS AND WEAKNESSES

In addition to the factors that they share in common, individual and family therapy each have specific strengths and weaknesses. These strengths and weaknesses are complementary and synergistic; the strengths of each approach add to those of the other and the weaknesses of each approach are compensated for by the other's strengths.

In the conceptualization of clinical problems, individually oriented approaches illuminate the significance of intrapsychic dynamics but minimize or neglect the significance of interpersonal dynamics. With family-oriented approaches, the opposite is the case. By integrating the two types of conceptualizations, a comprehensive model of individual and family dynamics can be developed.

In the area of clinical assessment, conjoint family interviews are uniquely valuable contexts for assessing interpersonal problems and strengths but are limited in their capacity to assess intrapsychic problems and strengths. Individual interviews have the opposite set of characteristics. Integration of the two approaches allows the therapist to conduct a comprehensive, multilevel clinical assessment.

The complementarity of individual and family therapy is also present in regard to therapeutic change processes. Individual therapy is a highly effective means for promoting intrapsychic changes but is limited in its capacity to promote interpersonal changes. Family therapy is highly effective in promoting interpersonal changes but is limited in its capacity to promote intrapsychic changes. Combining the two approaches maximizes the stimulation of both intrapsychic and interpersonal change processes, as well as the positive, growth-enhancing interactions between them.

## INTEGRATION

As described in detail in Chapter 3, individual and family therapy can be integrated in a number of different ways. Individual and family interviews can be utilized equally often (symmetrical integration) or one type of interview can be predominant (asymmetrical integration). Each therapy session can be conducted in one format only, or the two formats can be combined during the course of one meeting. The entire therapy can be conducted by one therapist, or the individual and family components can be divided between two therapists.

The overriding consideration in deciding on the type of integrative structure to use is the therapist's assessment of the specific problems, strengths, motivations, and resistances of the particular individuals and family. In order to make such an assessment, the therapist needs to recognize the importance of both intrapsychic and interpersonal dynamics, be able to conduct a comprehensive, multilevel clinical assessment, and be familiar with each of the different ways that individual and family therapy can be integrated.

In order to successfully implement an integrated treatment plan, the therapist needs to understand the importance of both intrapsychic and interpersonal change processes, be able to utilize both individually oriented and family-oriented therapeutic techniques, monitor the course of the therapy and make changes when indicated, and facilitate an effective, growth-promoting termination process.

## TRAINING IN INDIVIDUAL AND
## FAMILY THERAPY INTEGRATION

Learning to integrate individual and family therapy requires both didactic and experiential training. In this concluding section, a method for conducting such training will be outlined.

Initially, the focus is on didactic training. The major concepts and principles of each approach are presented and discussed. Then, methods for integrating the two approaches are delineated and illustrated with clinical examples and with audiotape, videotape, and role-play demonstrations.

The didactic training is followed by a period of supervised experiential training, during which the concepts and principles learned in the didactic phase are applied to trainees' cases. The supervisor monitors the trainees' clinical work via either process notes or tape recordings. In discussing this work, the supervisor reinforces constructive interventions, points out interventions that he or she believes are not constructive, suggests more effective alternatives, and explains the reasons for his or her suggestions.

Cases are followed over time so that the trainees can gain an understanding of the different phases of the therapy process, the different goals of each phase, and the different techniques that are most likely to be effective during each of these phases. Potential problems and ways to avoid them are discussed at length. When problems do arise, the discussion focuses on effective means for resolving them.

Reading is an integral part of the training process. While reading is not a substitute for systematic didactic and experiential training, it can be a stimulus for and an aid to such training. It is the author's hope that this book will be both a stimulus and an aid to the reader in his or her efforts to learn individual and family therapy integration.

# References

Achenbach, T.M. (1981). *Child behavior checklist*. Burlington, VT: University of Vermont.

Achenbach, T.M., & Edelbrock, C. (1981). *Youth self-report*. Burlington, VT: University of Vermont.

Aponte, H.J., & VanDeusen, J.M. (1981). Structural family therapy. In A.S. Gurman & D.P. Kniskern (Eds.), *Handbook of family therapy*. New York: Brunner/Mazel.

Babigian, H.M. (1985). Schizophrenia: Epidemiology. In H.I. Kaplan & B.J. Sadock (Eds.), *Comprehensive textbook of psychiatry/IV* (Vol. 1). Baltimore: Williams & Wilkins.

Baker, E.L. (1985). Psychoanalysis and psychoanalytic psychotherapy. In S.J. Lynn & J.P. Garske (Eds.), *Contemporary psychotherapies: Models and methods*. Columbus, OH: Chs. E. Merrill.

Barton, C., & Alexander, J.F. (1981). Functional family therapy. In A.S. Gurman & D.P. Kniskern (Eds.), *Handbook of family therapy*. New York: Brunner/Mazel.

Beck, A.T. (1976). *Cognitive therapy and the emotional disorders*. New York: International Universities Press.

Beitman, B.D., Goldfried, M.R., & Norcross, J.C. (1989). The movement toward integrating the psychotherapies: An overview. *American Journal of Psychiatry, 146*, 138–47.

Berman, S. (1979). The psychodynamic aspects of behavior. In J.D. Noshpitz (Ed.), *Basic handbook of child psychiatry* (Vol. 2). New York: Basic Books.

Bowen, M. (1978). *Family therapy in clinical practice*. New York: Jason Aronson.

Broder, E.A., & Hood, E. (1983). A guide to the assessment of child and family. In P.D. Steinhauer & Q. Rae-Grant (Eds.), *Psychological problems of the child in the family*. New York: Basic Books.

Canetto, S., Feldman, L.B., & Lupei, R. (1989). Suicidal persons and their partners. *Suicide and Life-Threatening Behavior, 19,* 237–248.

Carek, D. (1979). Individual psychodynamically oriented therapy. In J.D. Noshpitz (Ed.), *Basic handbook of child psychiatry* (Vol. 3, S. Harrison, Ed.). New York: Basic Books.

Chamberlain, C., & Steinhauer, P.D. (1983). Conduct disorders and delinquency. In P.D. Steinhauer & Q. Rae-Grant (Eds.), *Psychological problems of the child in the family*. New York: Basic Books.

Clifford, C., & Kolodny, R. (1983). Sex therapy for couples. In B. Wolman & G. Stricker (Eds.), *Handbook of family and marital therapy*. New York: Plenum.

Cohen, R.L. (1979). Assessment. In J.D. Noshpitz (Ed.), *Basic handbook of child psychiatry*. New York: Basic Books.

Ellis, A. (1973). *Growth through reason*. Palo Alto, CA: Science and Behavior Books.

Erikson, E.H. (1963). *Childhood and society*. New York: Norton.

Feldman, L.B. (1976a). Goals of family therapy. *Journal of Marriage and Family Counseling, 2,* 103–115.

Feldman, L.B. (1976b). Processes of change in family therapy. *Journal of Family Counseling, 4,* 14–22.

Feldman, L.B. (1976c). Strategies and techniques of family therapy. *American Journal of Psychotherapy, 30,* 14–28.

Feldman, L.B. (1976d). Depression and marital interaction. *Family Process, 15,* 389–395.

Feldman, L.B. (1979). Marital conflict and marital intimacy: An integrative psychodynamic-behavioral-systemic model. *Family Process, 18,* 69–79.

Feldman, L.B. (1982a). Dysfunctional marital conflict: An integrative interpersonal-intrapsychic model. *Journal of Marital and Family Therapy, 8,* 417–428.

Feldman, L.B. (1982b). Integrating behavioral and psychodynamic techniques in marital therapy. In A. Gurman (Ed.), *Questions and answers in the practice of family therapy* (Vol. 2). New York: Brunner/Mazel.

Feldman, L.B. (1985a). Integrative multilevel therapy: A comprehensive interpersonal and intrapsychic approach. *Journal of Marital and Family Therapy, 11,* 357–372.

Feldman, L.B. (1985b). *Family problems and strengths assessment.* Unpublished manuscript.

Feldman, L.B. (1988). Integrating individual and family therapy in the treatment of symptomatic children and adolescents. *American Journal of Psychotherapy, 42,* 272–280.

Feldman, L.B. (1989). Integrating individual and family therapy. *Journal of Integrative and Eclectic Psychotherapy, 8,* 41–52.

Feldman, L.B., & Pinsof, W.M. (1982). Problem maintenance in family systems—An integrative model. *Journal of Marital and Family Therapy, 8,* 295–308.

Finkelhor, D. (1984). *Child sexual abuse: New theory and research.* New York: Free Press.

Framo, J.L. (1981). The integration of marital therapy with sessions with family of origin. In A.S. Gurman & D.P. Kniskern (Eds.), *Handbook of family therapy.* New York: Brunner/Mazel.

Freud, A. (1933). *The ego and the mechanisms of defense.* New York: International Universities Press.

Freud, S. (1959). *Inhibitions, symptoms, and anxiety.* Standard edition (Vol. 20). London: Hogarth. (Original work published 1926).

Friedman, P.H. (1981). Integrative family therapy. *Family Therapy, 8,* 171–178.

Gardner, R.A. (1979). Helping children cooperate in therapy. In J.D. Noshpitz (Ed.), *Basic handbook of child psychiatry* (Vol. 3, S. Harrison, Ed.). New York: Basic Books.

Gill, M.M. (1982). *Analysis of transference.* New York: International Universities Press.

Goldfried, M.R. (1971). Systematic desensitization as training in self-control. *Journal of Consulting and Clinical Psychology, 37,* 228–234.

Goldfried, M.R., & Davison, G.C. (1976). *Clinical behavior therapy.* New York: Holt, Rinehart, & Winston.

Gordon, S.B., & Davidson, N. (1981). Behavioral parent training. In A.S. Gurman & D.P. Kniskern (Eds.), *Handbook of family therapy.* New York: Brunner/Mazel.

Greenspan, S.I. (1981). *The clinical interview of the child.* New York: McGraw-Hill.

Grinstein, A. (1983). *Freud's rules of dream interpretation.* New York: International Universities Press.

Gurman, A.S. (1981). Integrative marital therapy: Toward the development of an interpersonal approach. In S. Budman (Ed.), *Forms of brief therapy.* New York: Guilford.

Hafner, R.J. (1986). *Marriage and mental illness.* New York: Guilford.

Haley, J. (1976). *Problem-solving therapy.* San Francisco: Jossey-Bass.

Jackson, D.D. (1965). The study of the family. *Family Process, 4,* 1–20.

Jacobson, E. (1938). *Progressive relaxation.* Chicago: University of Chicago Press.

Jacobson, N.S. (1981). Behavioral marital therapy. In A.S. Gurman & D.P. Kniskern (Eds.), *Handbook of family therapy.* New York: Brunner/Mazel.

Jaffe, J.H. (1985). Opioid dependence. In H.I. Kaplan & B.J. Sadock (Eds.), *Comprehensive textbook of psychiatry/IV.* Baltimore: Williams and Wilkins.

Kempe, R.S., & Kempe, C.H. (1978). *Child abuse.* Cambridge, MA: Harvard University Press.

Kendall, P.C., & Braswell, L. (1985). *Cognitive-behavioral therapy for impulsive children.* New York: Guilford.

Kohut, H. (1971). *The analysis of the self.* New York: International Universities Press.

Kohut, H. (1977). *The restoration of the self.* New York: International Universities Press.

Kramer, C.H. (1980). *Becoming a family therapist: Developing an integrated approach to working with families.* New York: Human Sciences Press.

Kreindler, S., & Armstrong, H. (1983). The abused child and the family. In P.D. Steinhauer & Q. Rae-Grant (Eds.), *Psychological problems of the child in the family.* New York: Basic Books.

Lebow, J.L. (1984). On the value of integrating approaches to family therapy. *Journal of Marital and Family Therapy, 10,* 127–138.

Levant, R.F., & Haffey, N.A. (1981, Summer). Toward an integration of child and family therapy. *International Journal of Family Therapy,* 130–143.

Levine, S., Korenblum, M., & Golombek, H. (1983). Disorders commonly appearing first during adolescence. In P.D. Steinhauer & Q. Rae-Grant (Eds.), *Psychological problems of the child in the family.* New York: Basic Books.

Lipman, R.S., Covi, L., & Shapiro, A.K. (1977). The Hopkins symptom checklist (HSCL): Factors derived from the HSCL-90. *Psychopharmacology Bulletin, 13,* 43–45.

Luborsky, L. (1984). *Principles of psychoanalytic psychotherapy.* New York: Basic Books.

Malone, C.A. (1979). Child psychiatry and family therapy. *Journal of the American Academy of Child Psychiatry, 18*, 4–21.

Maruyama, M. (1968). The second cybernetics: Deviation amplifying mutual causal processes. In W. Buckley (Ed.), *Modern systems research for the behavioral scientist*. Chicago: Aldine.

McConville, B. (1983). Depression and suicide in children and adolescents. In P.D. Steinhauer & Q. Rae-Grant (Eds.), *Psychological problems of the child in the family*. New York: Basic Books.

Meichenbaum, D.H. (1977). *Cognitive behavior modification: An integrative approach*. New York: Plenum.

Meichenbaum, D.H. (1985). Cognitive-behavioral therapies. In S.J. Lynn & J.P. Garske (Eds.), *Contemporary psychotherapies: Models and methods*. Columbus, OH: Chs. E. Merrill.

Minuchin, S. (1974). *Families and family therapy*. Cambridge, MA: Harvard University Press.

Minuchin, S., & Fishman, H.C. (1981). *Family therapy techniques*. Cambridge, MA: Harvard University Press.

Moore, B., & Fine, B. (Eds.). (1968) *A glossary of psychoanalytic terms and concepts*. New York: American Psychoanalytic Association.

Moultrop, D. (1981). Toward an integrated model of family therapy. *Clinical Social Work Journal, 9*, 111–125.

Nadelson, C. (1978). Marital therapy from a psychoanalytic perspective. In T.J. Paolino & B.S. McCrady (Eds.), *Marriage and marital therapy*. New York: Brunner/Mazel.

Norcross, J.C., & Goldfried, M.R. (in press). *Handbook of psychotherapy integration*. New York: Basic Books.

Novaco, R.W. (1975). *Anger control: The development and evaluation of an experimental treatment*. Lexington, MA: Heath.

Perls, F.S. (1970). Four lectures. In J. Fagan & I.L. Shepherd (Eds.), *What is gestalt therapy?*. New York: Science and Behavior Books.

Pinsof, W.M. (1983). Integrative problem-centered therapy: Toward the synthesis of family and individual psychotherapies. *Journal of Marital and Family Therapy, 9*, 19–36.

Rimm, D.C., & Cunningham, H.M. (1985). Behavior therapies. In S.J. Lynn & J.P. Garske (Eds.), *Contemporary psychotherapies: Models and methods*. Columbus, OH: Chs. E. Merrill.

Robin, A.L., & Foster, S.L. (1989). *Negotiating parent-adolescent conflict: A behavioral-family systems approach*. New York: Guilford.

Rogers, C.R. (1980). *A way of being*. Boston: Houghton-Mifflin.

Rosenbaum, A., & O'Leary, K.D. (1986). The treatment of marital violence. In N.S. Jacobson & A.S. Gurman (Eds.), *Clinical handbook of marital therapy*. New York: Guilford.

Sager, C.J. (1981). Couples therapy and marriage contracts. In A.S. Gurman & D.P. Kniskern (Eds.), *Handbook of family therapy*. New York: Brunner/Mazel.

Sander, F. (1979). *Individual and family therapy: Toward an integration*. New York: Jason Aronson.

Segraves, R.T. (1982). *Marital therapy: A combined psychodynamic-behavioral approach*. New York: Plenum.

Shapiro, D. (1989). *Psychotherapy of neurotic character*. New York: Basic Books.

Stanton, M.D. (1981). Strategic approaches to family therapy. In A.S. Gurman & D.P. Kniskern (Eds.), *Handbook of family therapy*. New York: Brunner/Mazel.

Steinhauer, P.D. (1985). Beyond family therapy: Toward a systemic and integrated view. *Psychiatric Clinics of North America, 8*, 923–945.

Steinhauer, P.D., & Berman, G. (1983). Anxiety, neurotic, and personality disorders in children. In P.D. Steinhauer & Q. Rae-Grant (Eds.), *Psychological problems of the child in the family*. New York: Basic Books.

Sugarman, S. (1982). Combining family therapy with other clinical interventions. In A. Gurman (Ed.), *Questions and answers in the practice of family therapy*, Vol. 2. New York: Brunner/Mazel.

Vaillant, G.E., & Perry, J.C. (1985). Personality disorders. In H.I. Kaplan & B.J. Sadock (Eds.), *Comprehensive textbook of psychiatry/IV*. Baltimore: Williams and Wilkins.

Wachtel, E. (1987). Family systems and the individual child. *Journal of Marital and Family Therapy, 13*, 15–27.

Wachtel, E., & Wachtel, P. (1986). *Family dynamics in individual therapy*. New York: Guilford.

Wachtel, P.L. (1977). *Psychoanalysis and behavior therapy: Toward an integration*. New York: Basic Books.

Wachtel, P.L. (1985). Integrative psychodynamic therapy. In S.J. Lynn & J.P. Garske (Eds.), *Contemporary psychotherapies: Models and methods*. Columbus, OH: Chs. E. Merrill.

Walsh, F. (1983) Family Therapy: A Systemtic Orientation to Treatment. In A. Rosenblatt & D. Waldfogel (Eds.), *Handbook of Clinical Social Work*. San Francisco: Jossey-Bass.

Watzlawick, P., Weakland, J., & Fisch, R. (1974). *Change: Principles of problem formation and problem resolution*. New York: Norton.

Wegscheider, S. (1981). *Another chance: Hope and health for the alcoholic family*. Palo Alto, CA: Science and Behavior Books.

Weissman, M.M., & Boyd, J.H. (1985). Affective disorders: Epidemiology. In H.I. Kaplan & B.J. Sadock (Eds.), *Comprehensive text-book of psychiatry/IV*. Baltimore: Williams and Wilkins.

Weissman, M.M., & Paykel, E.S. (1974). *The depressed woman: A study of social relationships*. Chicago: University of Chicago Press.

Williams, L.H., Berman, H.S., & Rose, L. (1987). *The too precious child: The perils of being a super-parent and how to avoid them*. New York: Atheneum.

Wolpe, J. (1958). *Psychotherapy by reciprocal inhibition*. Stanford, CA: Stanford University Press.

# Name Index

# Subject Index